Challenges

Challenges

A Life of
Adventure for Charity

Dave Wellman

The Pentland Press
Edinburgh – Cambridge – Durham

First published in 1993 by
The Pentland Press Ltd
1 Hutton Close
South Church
Bishop Auckland
Durham

ISBN 1-85821-33-x

Typeset by Carnegie Publishing, 18 Maynard St., Preston
Printed and bound by Antony Rowe Ltd., Chippenham

Contents

National Spinal Injuries Centre

Jimmy Savile Stoke Mandeville
Hospital Trust, No.283127
Jimmy Savile Charitable Trust,
No. 326970

at Stoke Mandeville Hospital

Mandeville Road Aylesbury Bucks HP21 8AL

Tel: Aylesbury (0296) 315000

Date 19.8.92

Please reply to:-

"I've seen lots of lovely and lively people come and go.

Dave Wellman was lovely, lively and a fighter way back in 1951 when we both competed in the Tour of Britain Cycle Race.

Thank goodness he is still going as strong as ever, but this time he is fighting on behalf of the less fortunate.

A remarkable man with a fund of remarkable stories. I recommend this one to you".

SIR JAMES SAVILE Kt., OBE., KCSG

"PS - He beat me in 1951 and is still beating me today."

Preface

I HAVE OFTEN BEEN DESCRIBED as an adventurer. Throughout my life, it is true that I have always searched for challenges, never content with the soft option, or the easy route. I have often been asked *why* I do such things – especially of late, when my various exploits have been publicised and more people have been made aware of what I do. I don't know if I can provide any answers to the question, other than to say that it is in my nature, but I hope that I can share something of my experiences with those who would like to able to know a little more.

As well as various adventures earlier on in my life, I had, at the time of writing this book, also completed four major cycle rides for charity. I had ridden the length of Britain, from John O'Groats to Land's End; I had travelled to the Arctic Circle – and beyond – in Norway; I had taken my bicycle along mountain trails from Kathmandu to Everest Base Camp; and, most recently, I had ridden the length and breadth of Death Valley, in Nevada and California. All of these adventures had been undertaken alone (apart from the Everest trip, on which I was accompanied by the obligatory Sherpa guides), and carrying with me only a tent, a spare set of clothes and bicycle spares for emergencies. I had lived, for the most part, on twenty-four hour army rations, or bought food and drink along the way. I had slept under canvas; in wayside huts; out underneath the stars; and, on one occasion, spent a night sheltered under a rock in a driving blizzard in the foothills of the Himalayas.

Since most of these trips had been undertaken after I had taken retirement from full-time teaching, I have been labelled, by some, as the "Pedalling Pensioner".

I am now in my early sixties, a time when many people consider that they have completed their working life, and are beginning to wind down, and take it easy. For me, life is in many ways just starting. So much has opened up for me; I have discovered an enormous amount about different ways of living, different attitudes and beliefs, different cultures. I have also discovered a great deal about myself. I have pushed myself to the extremes of physical endurance. I have understood what it is like to be completely on your own, dependent only on your own resourcefulness for survival. I have been to places in the world that many people will only ever read about, and spoken with people whose lives have been far, far removed from my own. It has been a rich and rewarding time, and in the following pages I hope to be able to share just some of the experiences I have had.

Yet this book is not intended to be a boastful record of my achievements. I have never been one to bask in any sort of glory – far from it! Those that know me will testify that, although my life might have been richer for the adventures I've had, I have not (I hope!) changed beyond all recognition; and I feel that this could be for two very clear reasons.

The first is my motivation for undertaking these adventures. I have always felt restless, it is true, but I don't believe I would have ever had the urge to contemplate such ludicrous trips had it not been for the fact that the names of all the places I have visited in some way capture the imagination of people, and inspire them to donate money, or other forms of sponsorship, for various charities. It is difficult to give a precise sum when calculating the total amount of money these cycling trips have raised for various local charities, although it has been well into six figures in all. But I have not gained, financially, in any way myself – the reward for me comes from knowing how badly needed, and how well-deserved, this money is, by those whose whole lives are shadowed with suffering and disability.

The second reason is that I am aware of the fact that I am physically fit. I have, by nature, always been able to exert myself. I have always been keen on sport, of any description, and indeed taught the subject in school for a good twenty years of my life. I have also always been an enthusiastic cyclist, and in my early days used to race for Britain. This inherent ability is something I have always felt immensely grateful for. I consider my physical fitness to be a gift, in the same way that an artist has a gift for painting, or a pianist the gift to make music, and to be blessed with such a gift is a very humbling thought. To have a gift and not to use it is possibly the worst crime. To have a gift and to use it for personal gain achieves little. To my mind it has been my duty to make use of the gift I have been given in order to help, in some small way, those who have never been so fortunate. It is all luck. There but for the grace of God go I, as the saying goes. I feel immensely lucky, and immensely privileged, to have been blessed with the gift of good health, with strength, and physical fitness. I hope that the adventures described in this book have helped, in some way, to ease the burden for those who suffer, and who cannot physically partake in such things.

Of course, now I have had a taste for adventure I am going to find it difficult to stop. I find it hard to stay still for very long, and am always itching to be off on the next adventure, to meet the next challenge. Plans are already afoot, even as I write, for yet another mad scheme; I am hunting through libraries for information and writing letters to hundreds of potential sponsors. I have often been labelled "eccentric", one journalist even joked that I was some sort of superman, but I don't think I am either of those things. Just an ordinary chap with a bit of a yearning for adventure who has been given the opportunity to fulfil his dreams and help others along the way. I have written this book in order to bring people just a bit closer to sharing those adventures – and of course, all the proceeds will go towards charity, and provide (I hope) a little bit extra for those who really need it.

Chapter One

Beginnings

O N MONDAY 25 January 1993 I had the honour of being
invited to the Press Launch for the 1993 Milk Race in
Kent. The launch was a prestigious and rather glittering
event which took place at The Swan Hotel in Tunbridge Wells,
in the presence of an array of local dignitaries, decked out in their
formal chains of office for the important occasion – including the
Chairman of Sevenoaks District council, Ann Dawson, the
Mayor of Tunbridge Wells, Dennis Smith, and the Mayor of
Ashford, Cathy Rosson. They were all there to witness the
unveiling of the local route for the 1993 Milk Race, and to
announce the preparations taking place for the big day, when this
now celebrated cycling race around Britain was to pass through
the local town of Sevenoaks. From January onwards, I was to
spend many hours helping to prepare for the Milk Race, which
was due to pass through my home town at about 1.40 p.m. on
31 May 1993. The District Council were organising a day to
commemorate the event, and I was to be liaising in particular
with Mark Whyman and Mrs Margaret Drummond, in the
preparation of all sorts of spectacular and exciting activities –
including cycle races for junior, senior and novice riders around
Sevenoaks' town centre, and other races due to converge on one
of the town's main car parks. But the real crowd puller was of
course to be the Milk Race itself – a touring race which has
become almost as widely publicised here as its famous counter-
part across the Channel – and I was to be present in Sevenoaks
that day as a very privileged Guest of Honour.

When the day arrived, there was a wonderful atmosphere of excitement and anticipation in the often quite sleepy streets of Sevenoaks. As the time neared for the Race to pass through, the roads were lined with a thick crowd of spectators, jamming the pavements and all craning their necks for a glimpse of the racers. As anyone who has ever seen the Milk Race will know, the cavalcade of motor vehicles which heralds the approach of the cyclists can cause as much excitement for the spectators as the riders themselves. Their arrival is anticipated by Press Cars, First Aid Vehicles and Police Outriders, and by the blaring of horns, the flashing of lights, and the waving of flags. There is an excited murmur amongst the crowd, which evolves into a hum, and then a buzzing, and then cries of "They're coming! They're coming!"

Then, in a flash of colour and a whirr of bicycle wheels, the cyclists pass. The group moves almost as one body, muscular legs working rhythmically, wheels spinning in a blur of spokes, heads bent low over handlebars.

As I watched this group of athletic young men, in their glistening lycra gear and with their expensive, gleaming machines, intent only on the road passing by, I could not help but feel a small twinge of nostalgia.

It is many, many years since I have raced with such a group, and in such a manner. The gear might have changed a bit – there was no lycra in the old days, just a pair of shorts and a team jersey – and the racing bikes might have become more colourful, but the hearts and minds of those young men would be as one, and I knew precisely how each and every one of them would be feeling. There is nothing like it in the world, you know, speeding through the countryside using only the power of your muscles and the concentration of your mind to cover the miles, and the sense of achievement at the end of the day is unbelievable. You may be exhausted, but you are exhilarated, too, and the next morning there is nothing you want more than to be back on your bike, setting out once again, refreshed, relaxed and invigorated, and ready for another day's challenge.

My racing days are long gone, of course, although the memory lingers still, but I have not given up my cycling, neither have I stopped looking for challenges. The spirit of adventure, once roused, is difficult to put down, and I think that as long as my legs have the power to push on the pedals, I shall keep on going, wherever in the world I can ride my bike (and even to some places where riding is impossible!) and always on the lookout for something new and exciting to do; something just a little bit different, that no one in the world might have thought of doing before.

* * * * * *

I often think it was by chance that I took up cycling. It's always difficult to say, of course, but when I look back over the years I think I can probably pinpoint the precise moment that affected the course of my life; the moment that resulted in all those many years of excitement and adventure, as well as providing me with the opportunity to help others less fortunate than myself.

I left school in 1943, at the age of fourteen. My memories of those days which are supposed to be the happiest of one's life are vague; what I recall most vividly is that most of my lessons were conducted in an air raid shelter. I think, as youngsters, we had absolutely no idea of the seriousness of war, or of the danger. I was brought up in Bermondsey, London, and I remember that the morning route to school was often littered with debris and pieces of shrapnel from the previous night's raid. We collected shrapnel in the way that other lads, from other generations, or in other surroundings, might have collected conkers; hoarding them up and comparing them for size at school. The penalty, if caught, was six of the best, and I think we were all probably more afraid of the cane than we were of bombs falling on us. Such is innocence.

I was never one of the bright ones, and in the early years I came consistently bottom of the class. However, I was not happy with this state of affairs, and remember feeling determined to break away from this humiliating position, and pull myself up. I concentrated on working, and by sheer effort and determination struggled slowly towards the top. I have struggled since, with challenges of a far different nature, and I am proud to say that I have never, never given up, no matter how gruelling the task I might have set myself.

When I left school I went to work as an apprentice electrical engineer at the Port of London. My father had worked as a docker, as had his father before him, and it was taken for granted that I would continue with the family tradition. I was never very happy there, though; I felt restless and tied down. I was fourteen years old, but knew, even then, that there were other things that I wanted to be doing with my life. I think I have always been acutely aware of how easy it is to waste one's life, or not to grab opportunities as they present themselves. If I have ever been afraid of anything, it is the fear that I might fritter my life away. I was aware of this even at the age of fourteen, and it was then that I was to grab an opportunity that was to alter the course of events quite radically.

As well as working as an apprentice at the docks I also earned a bob or two by working as a paper boy for a time, delivering newspapers around Bermondsey. Labour was still in short supply, on account of the war, and so one of my duties was to ride to the railway station to collect all the newspapers, as there was no delivery to the newsagent's. This I did on a heavy, black, trades bicycle, with a large iron carrying grid on the front. It was a task I thoroughly enjoyed, especially on the outward trip, without the heavy bundles of papers loaded on the front and affecting my balance. One day, having completed this errand, I was pedalling home on my trusty old machine when I came across a group of cyclists on their flash racers, speeding down the road together in a lively, noisy cluster. I decided to test myself, and see if I could keep pace with them. Pushing down hard on the pedals, I gave the old girl all I'd got, and slowly gained ground on the group. Not only did I keep up, but I also managed to overtake them, and as I pedalled furiously past I could hear their laughter and cheers.

We got chatting, inevitably, and they poured much scorn on the bicycle I was riding.

"Why don't you get yourself a decent bike and come and join a cycling club?" one of them asked.

"Oh, I can't afford things like that!" I laughed, dismissing the idea completely. Money was tight, in those days, and there was no room for luxury. Cycling, for me, was definitely to be considered a luxury.

However, George Philips, a keen member of the group, and a generous and very affable soul, offered to help piece together a machine for me; he reckoned that between them they had enough spare parts to constitute a reasonably respectable model. George was as good as his word; I arranged to meet the lads the following Sunday and was overwhelmed when they proudly produced a bicycle for me. We set out together, that day, and I have to say, I never looked back. I had the time of my life and discovered, to my delight, that cycling was definitely for me!

George and the rest of the group were very encouraging, and there began a very enjoyable and fulfilling period, when I discovered, for the first time, the great pleasure to be had from distance cycling. We met regularly, every Sunday, and would set off for a different location each week, sometimes covering between 100 and 150 miles. We explored in every possible direction, although a favourite jaunt was always to the coast and back. There was some serious cycling, and of course a certain amount of larking about, but I was always able to keep pace with them all, and would often sail out in front, just as I had done that morning on my heavy old delivery bike. After some weeks had passed, George and some of the others said they thought I should enter a race. Again I refused, initially, assuming that this would mean a financial outlay. However small, it would have been out of the question to actually *pay* for something I enjoyed doing. But I discovered that all I needed was a licence, which, in the end, I duly procured. With this licence I became an official member of the British League of Racing Cyclists, which at the time was considered to be quite a rebel organisation. They were taking over from the National Cycling Union and the Road Time Trial Association, and it was the British League which really set up organised cycle racing in this country. Eventually the League amalgamated with the NCU to form the British Cycling Federation – but let me assure you that politics can enter the world of cycling just as bitterly as in any other sphere, and it was some while before the dust settled. Anyway, politics apart, I was soon the proud holder of a BLRC Licence, entitling me to race officially. I must say I was very doubtful indeed that I was up to the standard of any of the others. I was also invited to become an official member of George's group – the newly formed Polhill Racers. It didn't cost me anything, and as there didn't seem to be anything to lose, I decided to join. I still have that licence to this day. It may be a little thin and faded now, and somewhat worn around the edges, but it still reminds me of the pride I felt to be acknowledged for the first time as a true cyclist.

My first race was at Crystal Palace. I was still riding the bike that George and the others had given me, and I knew full well it was not really up to the proper standard. At the starting post, all the cyclists were lined up busily checking over their machines, and making last minute adjustments and preparations. I hadn't got a *clue* what I was supposed to be doing, and just stood waiting nervously with my bike, feeling very self-conscious. At last we were off, heads down and pedalling as fast as we could around

15 laps of the track – a distance of about 26 miles. It was not far, but it was fast. It seemed to pass in a complete blur. I don't remember anything at all apart from watching for the sign that I had passed another lap, and the concentration on pushing as fast as I could to make those wheels spin. I didn't win this race, but I finished in a respectable position in the main group. I felt excited and exhilarated, and I had enjoyed every moment. My cycling career had begun.

Life continued in a fairly easy manner. I was still working at the docks, but lived for the weekends when I could set out for the country on my bicycle. After that first race at Crystal Palace I took part in various events, and gradually began to improve my performance. At last I felt I had discovered something that I really wanted to do! But then, one ill-fated morning in 1948, an envelope arrived on the mat which was to change things completely. I had been called up for National Service, and was to join the Royal Artillery. This was a bit of a blow. I have to admit that I was a very reluctant serviceman, and at first regarded the time I had to spend in the army only as an irritating nuisance, getting in the way of the things that I wanted to be doing. Just as it had started so well, I felt that my cycling career had been called to an abrupt halt, and this seemed very unfair. However, once I had joined I was determined to give it my best shot – I have never been one to do things by halves.

After twelve weeks' training, which seemed to consist mainly in a lot of square-bashing, I was despatched with the 2nd AGRA (Army Group Royal Artillery) to the Middle East, on the troopship "Empress of Australia". It was before the Suez Crisis, with no real possibility of action or excitement, but plenty of dull routine ahead. On board ship I was required to police the troops and help maintain law and order. We sailed via Gibraltar and Malta, to the Suez Canal. I had never really been anywhere before in my life, and it felt exciting to be travelling, and glimpsing new places, however briefly. We were to be based just outside Ismalia, which is on the banks of the canal, south of Port Said. Here we were under canvas, and the conditions were not that pleasant – it was blisteringly hot and dry during the day, I remember, and freezing cold at night. Although it had certainly felt quite exciting to travel, and to be on the move, I certainly did not enjoy standing still. There was very little military activity here at this time; I was one of a group operating radar equipment to monitor aircraft. The work was punctuated by various exercises, but it all felt rather futile, and, enclosed in the army camp in the stifling heat, and with the even more stifling company, I began to feel restless, and in need of something to do. Not one to be daunted by the prospect of anything different or unusual, I went to see my colonel one day, with the proposal that I take six men on a charity walk across the Sinai Desert, from Port Said to Aqaba, a distance of some 200 miles. Money from the trip would go to benefit war widows. The colonel agreed readily, and I was given permission to prepare for the expedition. The next few days were spent busily gathering supplies and provisions, studying maps and talking to local Arab guides.

The walk took us fourteen days in all. The Sinai Desert, for those whose geography is hazy, forms the triangle of land between the two "snail's horns" of the Red Sea. There are no roads or paths across the desert – we found our way in the time-honoured tradition, according to the stars and the sun. Even now I like to check my ability to do this by looking up at the sky – usually for a joke when some bright spark in one of my classes at school asks innocently for the time, even though he has a timepiece as wide as a tennis ball on his wrist. The joke ends up being on *him* when I assure him quite accurately of the hour, merely by glancing out of the window!

Although the desert consisted of sand, sand, and yet more sand, the terrain was quite varied. At times we would be struggling up huge, soft mounds of dry, shifting sand, and yet elsewhere we walked easily across firm, compact sand which formed a surface hard enough to play football on. We carried heavy packs, with all our regulation army gear, and twenty-four-hour rations. None of today's lightweight equipment in those days. We kept up a fair pace, but at time it was hard, the sun beating down mercilessly and every step growing heavier and heavier. Beads of sweat would gather on your forehead and drip down into your eyes. We were well covered, to avoid sunburn. You would have done anything for a patch of shade, just to escape from that scorching heat. Then, as night fell, the temperature dropped and there was a complete contrast. Suddenly the sun would dip behind the horizon – there was only ever about half an hour at most of anything you could call 'evening' – and quickly the heat would disperse. As we crawled into our bags at night I can often recall shivering and looking forward to the heat of the next morning.

As we were setting up camp every night we were regularly visited by groups of curious Bedouin Arabs, who travelled across the desert on camels. They would approach cautiously at first, and then, recognising us as British soldiers, would grin and embark on the routine patter:

"Look sir I have very good bargain. This one especially for you."

And out would come the trinkets. They pestered and pestered with grim determination until one of our group would at last relent – but the story did not end there. You had to bargain and haggle, with ritualistic solemnity, until a suitable compromise was reached and then there were broad smiles all round. Then they would wish us well, and mount their patiently waiting camels, which, with a look of bored disdain, would stagger to their feet and set off across the harshly lit sands, until they were mere specks on the horizon. I remember one particular Bedouin who said his name was Ramsee; he was a real fly-by-night, who had the look of a true spiv about him – I would not have bought a second-hand car off this fellow, let alone anything else! Ramsee insisted on telling us how poor he was, and when he had succeeded in making us all feel sorry for him he swiftly produced a whole array of goods to sell. We soon learnt to be very cautious.

The expedition lasted a fortnight in all. Apart from the itinerant Bedouins, there was little to vary the days. Sometimes an army jeep or two, trundling across the sand and creating clouds of dust billowing behind. Endless marching, day after day, ever onwards towards our goal. Spirits were high, though; we all got on well, and learnt much, during those long days, about team spirit and the qualities needed to work with others. It was a marvellous feeling to reach Aqaba at last, where the RS Rangers were encamped. They had been warned of our arrival and we were all given a warm welcome. We were fed and watered, and once cleaned and rested we were also provided with transport back across the desert. It was certainly a great relief to be covering that vast, arid expanse in just a few hours instead of two weeks, and in the relative comfort of an army jeep!

I thoroughly enjoyed the challenge of this little adventure, the planning and preparation involved as well as the walk itself. I also felt I had the ability to lead and organise, and found this very satisfying. Other activities and sports followed: I took up hockey and played for the army, and also started swimming, soon becoming the Royal Artillery Canal Zone freestyle champion. All in all, army life was turning out to be far better than I had at first anticipated, and it was at this time that I began to discover my abilities for a diversity of sporting activities. I was really missing my cycling, though, and now began to seek out a bike in earnest. Bicycles were a rare sight in that part of the world, but I had heard of the "Bukshee Wheelers" – a cycling club in Cairo which had been formed by servicemen during the war. "Bukshee" meant "nothing" or "for free" in army Arabic; presumably because "nothing" was what those chaps had started out with. Anyway I had heard of the club, which meant, as far as I was concerned, that there must still be bikes around, somewhere. I was lucky enough to be able to speak a little of the language, and I think this helped me considerably in getting away with all sorts of things that I wanted to do, that other people might have found more difficult.

At last, I found someone who had a bike, and after some wheeling and dealing, was able to persuade them to part with it. It was a real wreck, but I managed to align the wheels, adjust the handlebars and straighten a few spokes. I was not convinced of its reliability, but was determined to have one ride, at least, and so I set out alone one day, heading south-west from Port Said on the road to Cairo. It was a glorious feeling to be pedalling along the road again, even though the scenery was most unfamiliar, the climate unpleasantly hot, and the machine I was riding far from comfortable! I was not as stiff as I might have been, what with all the sport on top of the regular army training, and I made it to Cairo without too much difficulty. Here I cycled all the way to the Pyramids, which are just outside the city. They are certainly an impressive sight, rising formidably out of the desert sand. I had some strange looks from people: the usual mode of transport around here was either on donkey or camel, and an Englishman on an old bicycle certainly merited a few hard stares, both from locals and other tourists. King Faruk was in power at this time, the Suez Crisis was brewing, which meant that there were not many tourists, but it was always necessary to be quite careful. I did not linger in Cairo, but felt relieved to have had the chance to ride again, and reassure myself that the old muscles were all still in place.

When I left the army in 1950, I returned to England to live with my uncle, in Bromley, south London. It took a while to get used to civilian life again, after the discipline and camaraderie of the army – and Bromley was certainly a far cry from Port Said – but it was sheer joy to return to my old, familiar, comfortable bicycle, and I began riding regularly, every day, in order to get back to the speeds and distances I had been capable of before.

I decided to take a job as a barrow boy, shouting my wares in East Street, which is just off the Walworth Road in Camberwell. I helped out on a stall selling fruit and veg – and the very amenable stallholder allowed me as much time off as I wanted, and whenever I wanted. As far as I was concerned, this was the perfect job, giving me plenty of time to concentrate on my cycling, and enter races whenever, and wherever, I had the chance. I was training regularly now, and entering – and winning – more and more. In the regular rides I still enjoyed with Polhill, I used to "burn them off" – leave the group way behind and sit out comfortably and easily in front. This was a technique that I used most often when I was racing, and it seemed to earn me a reputation. I suppose that it was because of this that I was selected, in 1951, to take part in the first ever Tour of Britain – an event sponsored by the Daily Express. These days this event is more commonly known as the Milk Race.

Chapter Two

Tour of Britain 1951

I N 1950 the *Daily Express* were still organising their annual Air Race – an event for light aircraft that took place across the south coast of England but 1950 was the last year for this spectacular event. As the Editor of the newspaper explained at the time, very few *Express* readers had ever flown in an aeroplane, but nearly 100% of their readers had, at one time or another in their lives, ridden a bicycle. It was this factor that persuaded the newspaper to abandon their sponsorship of the air race, and to initiate instead an event that was to be based on the famous Tour de France. The inaugural *Daily Express* Tour of Britain Cycle Race was planned to take place in August 1951 – and I had been selected to ride for the South London team. There were six cyclists in each team, of which the four best were to be counted at the end of the race.

At the start of the race the 140 cyclists gathered in Hyde Park, London, amid a hubbub of noise and excited chatter, and the repeated clicking of newspaper cameras. It was here, amongst what must have seemed to an outsider to look like absolute chaos, that I met a young man who was riding with the North of England team. He had an infectious laugh and a very lively sense of humour; his name was Jimmy Savile. Although I had met him in previous races, it was on this first ever Tour of Britain that I really felt I got to know Jim well. I was also, during the course of the race, to become aware of his deeply generous spirit, his great sense of fun, and above all his extremely selfless nature.

This first Tour of Britain took place over 14 days, and covered 1,400 miles in all. We set off from London on 19 August, and returned on 1 September, having passed through Brighton, Bournemouth, Plymouth, Weston, Cardiff, Wolverhampton, Morecambe, Glasgow, Newcastle, Scarborough, Nottingham and Norwich – often cycling over 100 miles a day. The race was very widely publicised, and I must say it was a very great honour to be taking part. All along the route thousands of people would line the streets, whole schools often turning out to wave and cheer as we sped past, no matter what time of day. Wherever we stopped, we were treated like celebrities, with local newspapers and television covering the event, and people surrounding us everywhere.

It is a fantastic feeling to become totally absorbed in one activity for that length of time. I felt as if I almost became part of my bike, and I certainly did not think, or talk, about anything else. A great spirit of friendship builds up between all those taking part in an event like this, and together we became like an exclusive club. Every night we would be booked in to a hotel. I would go and find my room and just collapse on the bed, too exhausted to do anything for a while. A masseur was always on hand to rub our legs, using the friction method of massage to ease the muscles – it is certainly a marvellous sensation. Then I would take a refreshing shower, and usually wander down to the dining room to have a meal with the others. Here the talk was *always* about bikes: we would talk about gears, about equipment, about any repairs or adjustments that had to be made, about tactics in the race. Today's performance was analysed in depth, and the prospects for the morrow discussed in full. It must have been very boring for any outsider, but for those of us taking part, it was something you could not have enough of. Our hearts, minds and spirits were concentrated with one accord on the events of the day. Every evening we would wait avidly for news of the race on the television; being the first race it was given very good coverage, and we would always raise a cheer if any of us got a mention. Then it was early to bed every evening, and straight to

First on left – a member of the winning team.

sleep. No matter how hard I had worked that day, I woke without fail feeling fresh and invigorated in the morning, ready for the punishment of the next day.

The race was divided into stages, and the winner of each stage would be awarded a small prize. I was hoping to earn a few bob in this way, as I was (as usual) completely broke at the time. After the first seven days had passed, however, I had not won a penny, and was beginning to feel rather despondent. We were on the Morecambe to Glasgow stretch of the race – a distance of 160 miles – it had been raining steadily for a while and my spirits were flagging. I found myself cycling alongside Jimmy Savile, and we began chatting.

"Dunno about you, Jim," I said, "but I'm skint."

With a twinkle in his eye, Jimmy said he would help me win the next stage of the race, and earn a bit of money. I listened

Front right. A quick gear change, and we're off once more.

intently to the scheme he came up with. Speaking quietly so that the others would not overhear the tactics, Jimmy said he would make a spurt ahead, and told me to follow. He then instructed me to pretend to "whip him up" and allow the rest of the group to think we were just fooling around. Not having won anything so far I was not going to be considered a serious threat by any of them.

I followed Jim's plan, and was duly ignored by the rest of the group, who obviously were not at all bothered by the simple barrow boy larking about with the joker Jimmy Savile. In front of us lay Shap Fell, a long, steep climb and one of the toughest stretches of the whole course. It was still raining as Jim and I began the ascent, still just out in front of the others, and still pretending to fool about; but then we rounded a corner, and momentarily disappeared from view. It was then that the fooling stopped, and together Jimmy and I put on a real spurt. He encouraged me all the way, and we really gave it all we'd got, working "bit by bit" – that is to say, taking it in turns to ride in front, with the one behind being in the lee of the other. We must have been at least five minutes ahead of the main group, and were really making good time, but then Jimmy "blew up" – he had had enough and said he could go on no further, leaving me to carry on while he waited for the others to catch up. I continued pushing hard up the steep hill, encouraged by Jimmy's enthusiasm and words of support. I was first up Shap Fell that day, and proudly received the prize money of £13 – quite a fortune in those days. As for Jim? Well, he just as proudly came last – although he has joked with me since that I have never given him his share of the prize money! He retired after that stretch of the race, but the *Daily Express* were reluctant to let him go, so he ended up as one of the announcers, amusing spectators with his cheery patter as they waited excitedly for the race to pass. An early foray into the world of entertainment from which Jimmy never looked back!

I continued on to Glasgow, still keeping out in front of the group. As I neared the finishing line of that stretch of the race I was joined by three professional cyclists (known as "Independents"); I tagged on with them for a while but they were too fast for me and I dropped behind them. I arrived in Glasgow in fourth position, but the first amateur, which was a great honour, and quite a personal achievement for me.

Our South London team won that first amateur Tour of Britain. As a member of that winning team, I certainly felt very proud and I think it was then that I realised that I was going to be a sportsman all my life. I remember I was billed as a hero by the Press, mostly on account of my winning the 160-mile Morecambe–Glasgow stretch, and the opportunities ahead of me seemed, at that time, limitless. Some of these were to prove more serious than others.

Recognize this dapper fellow?

After the cycling season was over that year, in 1951, I had time enough on my hands to take an active part in the "social" season. The winter months were taken up with serious training, of course, but 1951 was also the year of the Festival of Britain. As part of the nationally celebrated event I remember making several

Warming up in the Time Trials for the Tour of Britain. Jimmy Savile keeps an eye on events and provides the commentary. I'm the one on the bike.

personal appearances, pedalling as fast as I could round a large arena on the South Bank, in London, in front of quite a large audience.

After this I went on to take part in several important races. One I remember in particular was a two-day event in Bournemouth, in the 1952 season.

The race covered about 250 miles in total, and took part in two stages. Because I could not afford any other means of transport, I cycled down to the start – a distance of another 120 miles – and then of course cycled back home again after the race was over. I succeeded in winning the first day of the race, and had the honour of being presented to the Mayor, amongst other formalities. The fact that I had won, however, meant that I had to work even harder the next day, for I was then a marked man. The tension

Setting out on the Bournemouth two-day event. I'm on the right.

Barrow boy Wellman does his nut. In the lead during a race at Brands Hatch.

was mounting as the race drew to a close; I was out in front with five others, and we all sprinted the last few miles. I crossed the finishing line first, to resounding cheers and thunderous applause; it was a wonderful moment, and one which I shall never forget. I was given a considerable amount of coverage in the media after that, and realised that I was beginning to make quite a name for myself. One newspaper reported that:

"Wellman, after ten miles, got up to his old, well-worn tactic of 'doing his nut' ahead of the field …'Barrow Boy' Wellman had at last got out in front – and stayed there." Someone, at some time, had found out my occupation, and the name stuck. Throughout the whole of my cycling career I was always known affectionately as The London Barrow Boy.

Most of my life was now taken up with racing. I would train hard throughout the week, and spend every weekend out distance cycling or taking part in some race. It was after the two-day event in Bournemouth that another milestone occurred: I was selected to ride for England. I now embarked on a period of International racing which was, of course, an immense honour, and introduced me to all sorts of new experiences and opportunities. I felt very privileged indeed when I wore the England jersey for the first time, as part of the team taking part in the 14-day Tour of Flanders Cycle Race.

This race covered a distance of some 1,500 miles, over very rough, poorly maintained, cobbled roads. One hundred and thirty-nine top international riders were taking part, including myself and two others in the England team – Peter Hayward and Graham Vines. The race was divided up into various sections, and there was much local support. In some towns, shopkeepers would put up prize money to be awarded to the first cyclist past their shop, and I won two of these myself. My final position was 38th, which I was pleased with, and I was delighted to receive a small trophy which was awarded to all those who finished the race.

From Flanders, Graham Vines and myself were flown straight over to Ireland, where we were joined by Brian Robinson to form the England team riding in the international "An Tostal". A race of over 400 miles, this was again a team event, and the three of us won the First Team Award. One amusing tale I recall was that some of us taking part in the race were asked to help in a promotional campaign being organised by Philips, who were marketing their electric shavers. We had to line up at the start of the race, on our bikes, and pretend to shave, whilst somebody filmed us, which resulted in a lot of merriment and banter between those of us taking part. As amateurs we were not allowed to be paid, but it was worth it nonetheless!

My status as an International Racing Cyclist was now confirmed, and after the An Tostal I took part in many one-day races, both at home and on the continent. It was àt this time that I first encountered one of the less appealing aspects of any competitive sport – the drugs element. Those who indulged took something that was then known as "Go Fast", and I witnessed participants blatantly injecting themselves in the changing rooms before the start of the race. I believe it was strychnine that they were using, which can be poisonous, but in small doses acts as a stimulant. But some people would resort to using dried horse's blood, or dried bananas – anything they could lay their hands on that might improve their performance. The problem was recognised, and acknowledged, but the only deterrent from the organisers was to announce that anyone found using drugs would be denied anaesthetic if they had to be hospitalised. The official line was much more casual than it is these days, but then I suppose the full implications of the problem had not been realised. I have to say it saddens me; those that I knew were taking drugs never seemed to last very long, and I believe that one chap actually lost his life as a result. To me it seems that they can have no confidence in their own ability, which is a great shame.

Confidence certainly was not something that I lacked in any way. My cycling was going from strength to strength and I was busy all the time, whether in training or actually racing. I was managing to scrape a living through taking part in cycle races now, but I wasn't exactly rolling in it. I remember one time turning up at Dover, to catch the ferry to the continent, with only £1 10s. in my pocket. At that time there was a minimum amount that you had to have on you, in order to leave the country; although I can't remember the exact amount, I remember quite clearly that £1 10s. was definitely below the legal limit. I was full of confidence then, however, and managed somehow to persuade the customs men that I would win enough to pay my way. I have never been one to worry too much about where the next meal will come from – I'm certain something will always turn up, and I'm sure that thinking positively is half the battle!

* * * * * *

I have in my possession today three small medals, all dated 1953, awarded for various "tandem-paced" events. Tandem-pacing is rare, these days – possibly it is something that has died out altogether, which is a shame, because the tandem-paced races which were held at Herne Hill Cycle Track were certainly colourful and lively events. For those unfamiliar with this particular aspect of the sport, tandem-paced cycling involves cycling just behind two tandem bikes which are, of course, generally faster than one bike over a shorter distance. For a small fee you can hire your own tandem, with riders, and the trick is to follow this as it speeds around the track. As the tandem riders tire, the tandem withdraws from the circuit, and another tandem enters to take its place. Broke as usual, I could not ever afford to fork out for my own tandem. I recall in one

Tandem-paced race. Herne Hill 1953.

of the races – the National Cyclists Union Championship, on 17 June 1955 – I had to tag along behind another competitor who was following his own tandem. After several laps of the circuit I took up with two tandems belonging to a chap who had pulled out of the race, and I ended up in third position, and also breaking the Tandem-Pace 25-mile record.

There are many who will recall the 1950s as being the "Golden Age", not only of tandem-paced cycling, but also of the cinema. As well as some splendid Hollywood movies, an evening's entertainment at the pictures was made complete by some kind of live show, during the intermission between films, or after the newsreel. After all the publicity I had received from my cycle racing, it came about, in the late fifties, that my short-lived show-business career was to take off. I was offered the chance by ABC Cinemas to take part in an act that was to be presented in their picture houses throughout the London area as part of the interval entertainment. Not one to turn down an opportunity, I accepted the offer, and thus became a professional entertainer, with Monty Condor, of Condor Cycles, as my manager. The act entailed sitting on a specially designed bicycle, fixed on a set of rollers (you could say this was the prototype of the exercise bike!), and pedalling as fast as I could on this machine, with the aim of reaching 100 m.p.h. As the lights went down, and the organ rose, I would appear on stage and climb aboard the glittering machine, a spotlight focusing on me clad in my shorts and England racing jersey. A "masseur" would come on and rub my legs before I mounted the bike, and the audience would cheer as I pedalled faster and faster. I never made it to 100 m.p.h. (the fastest speed I reached was 94), but I shall always remember the fantastic atmosphere in the cinemas, and the audiences who were busily eating ice creams before the next film, and watching Dave Wellman make a fool of himself in front of the crowd!

This job did not last long, but while I was employed by ABC Cinemas I was, officially, a professional – that is to say, I was making money from my cycling, however unconventional that may have been – and so it was that I missed out on what was perhaps one of the greatest opportunities of my life – the chance to ride for England in the 1956 Melbourne Olympic Games. It was, of course, an immense honour even to have been considered for the Olympics, and I am very proud indeed that my name was put forward. At this point in my life I was cycling about 300 miles a week in training. I had not competed in any serious competitions since 1953, and in order to get back to top-class international standard I would have had to have put in about 800 miles a week, including some non-stop 100-mile runs. However, because I had given up my amateur status in order to work for ABC Cinemas, my name was, in the end, discounted. The fact that, as a professional, I could no longer ride for England is one of those things that I regard as fate, really. Other events were to take over in my life; I did not abandon cycling or sport altogether, but from then on things were to take a slightly different course, and other priorities took their place. Perhaps the most important of these was the fact that, in 1957, I met my future wife, Olive.

Being awarded the Lanterne Rouge, 1957.

Chapter Three

Teaching

O LIVE ALWAYS ASSURES ME that it was love at first sight –
although I don't remember her saying so at the time!
We met at a Cycling Club Social, where I had gone for
the evening with some friends. Our courtship began at a time
when I was still riding professionally, but also supplementing the
income I made from cycling with some part-time teaching. This
meant that my weeks and weekends were generally full, and I
was away from home quite a bit. By the end of 1958 I had given
up racing altogether, but not before I had ridden once more in
the Tour of Britain Cycle Race. My achievement was somewhat
different this time – I had the honour of coming last! This is not,
in fact, quite the humiliation that it sounds. There is a time limit
imposed upon the final stages of the race, which means that posi-
tions will only be awarded to those who cross the finishing line
within the allocated time. A straggler who falls, say, half an hour
behind the main group does not, therefore, get counted at all. But
the chap who, usually by accident rather than design, is the last to
cross the line within the designated time is made a great fuss of.
And so it was that, achieving this exalted position in the 1957
Tour of Britain, I was awarded the "Lanterne Rouge", with all
the ceremony befitting one who had come first, rather than last.
Just one of the idiosyncratic traditions of the cycling fraternity!

Although I still enjoyed distance cycling, I knew, then, that
my racing days were over. I was just not getting enough time to
train. However, I made several long trips just for pleasure. In '58
I cycled with Jimmy May and Vic Barnes to San Sebastian, on

the west coast of France, and the following year rode all the way
through France and down, through Italy, to Sicily and Mount
Etna – a trip which took six weeks in all. Olive got used to my
being away from home, on my bike, from our earliest time together. She didn't mind too much then, and luckily still does not
mind now. Of course I always promote her, wherever I go – she
is chief cook and bottle washer, head gardener, and a dab hand
at rearing chickens!

On my return from my 1959 trip I opened a cycle and electrical shop in Bromley. I was able to use my name to sell goods in
the shop, and the business made very good money, but at the end
of two years I began to feel depressed by the routine that it
entailed. One evening I spent thinking through things; trying to
decide what I should do with my life, and what direction I
wanted it to take. I felt that I was becoming trapped in a lifestyle
I did not really care for. My greatest fear was that I might sink
into apathy; that earning a regular and reliable income would
eventually mean that I would lose all motivation, and that I
would become incapable of doing anything other than watching
the TV, sleeping and eating. Perhaps my main driving force has
always been my determination not to waste my life; on that evening
in 1961 I began to feel that this was happening, and, realising that
it was up to me to do something about this, I went along to the
shop the very next day and offered to sell the business to the
manager. He agreed readily, and, although I had now given up cycle
racing for good, and had little else other than the teaching to bring
in any money, I felt immense relief at relinquishing the business,
and knew for certain that I had done the right thing.

I continued my part-time teaching, working as a football coach
and judo instructor in primary schools throughout London. I
also took up weight training at Crystal Palace. On 12 October
1962 Olive and I were married, and life began to assume a quiet
rhythm as I now settled down to bring up a family. Our eldest
son, David, was born in 1963, a day remembered by many for a

At work in the shop.

less happy reason, as it was on the same day that President Kennedy was shot. Two years later Tessa appeared, and then we had two four-year gaps between our last two children, Graham (1969) and Richard (1973). Throughout the sixties I continued with my part-time teaching jobs. We were living in Bromley at the time, and I was earning just enough to keep the family, and at the same time have a certain amount of variety in my own life. By 1969, however, I decided that I should find a permanent post with a more secure income. I scoured the job advertisements in the newspaper, and came across a vacancy for a full-time sports instructor at Wilson's Grammar School, in Camberwell. I applied for the job and was given an interview by the head, Mr Friskney, a very amiable chap who agreed to take me on. He introduced me to the rest of the staff, and to Bill Sollis, the head of PE at the school.

So began my first permanent teaching job, and during the next six years I began to feel quite settled and content, dividing my time between teaching and the family. I had given up my cycling, but in my time at Wilson's I acquired all sorts of skills and learnt a great deal, thanks mainly to Bill, who was an excellent instructor. He guided me carefully every step of the way, and set a marvellous example. I firmly believe that education is not merely to do with teaching children about certain subjects, but also involves helping them to lead happy and fulfilling lives. Everyone at that school was tremendous: the head, the staff, the boys and even the cooks, who all worked together in a friendly and very congenial environment. As a full-time PE Instructor, I was required to teach many sports that were unfamiliar to me. The school was always most supportive, and I was sent on several specialist training courses which helped me to become quite an all-rounder where sporting events were concerned. I still have in my possession a whole folder stuffed full of certificates for volleyball, fencing, weight-training, cricket, swimming, badminton, judo (I attained the Black Belt First Dan within two years), and last but not least, a certificate qualifying me to act as a Referee in Bicycle Polo.

There are several advantages of being a PE Teacher, which is quite unlike any other specialist teaching post. Children behave differently in PE lessons, and often those less academically skilled have the opportunity to shine in ways that are otherwise denied them. Often you get to see a side of the children that those stuck in the classroom rarely see. Sometimes this is good; at other times, of course, PE can bring out the worst in youngsters. There will always be those who dislike sport intensely, and will seek every opportunity they can to avoid the class, and inevitably, too, the Shirkers, who will go to any lengths to avoid *anything*. In order to be excused PE at Wilson's, it was necessary for the child to bring a note. The beginning of a PE class was always delayed for a few minutes, whilst these grubby little notes were produced

– or not, as the case may be. The content of these notes always made amusing reading, although I had to be careful never to let a glimmer of a smile cross my lips when reading them.

"Please excuse David from PE as he has injured his toes."

"Could Paul be excused from games as he has been rather chesty?"

"Michael is still unable to do sports until his results have come through."

"Please excuse Terry from games until his knee is better."

"Please excuse Richard from PE today; he had an accident on his roller skates yesterday and has cuts and bruising on his right side and it feels very uncomfortable."

"Please excuse Bobby from games today as he slept badly and woke up with a slightly stiff neck."

"May Jason be excused PE as he has a heavy cold"

And the classic, which I shall always remember:

"Dear Sir,

Sorry Stephen cannot do games today as his left foot is not right yet. Thank you."

The list could go on, but, for the few who were reluctant to participate, there were the many who enjoyed their sport. Seeing some of those young children try, and succeed, and work together in teams and above all discover, as I had done, the rewards to be had from physical exertion, was certainly a reward in itself for me.

In January 1975, Wilson's School was moved to Wallington, in Surrey. Ever since I had started teaching I had worked with London children, and I did not want to change now, so, reluctantly, I left Wilson's and all the friends I had made there, and found a new post at the Strand School, in Brixton. Here I stayed for the next three years, and then in 1978 I sat an exam to qualify for a place on a teacher-training course at the University of London. I passed the exam, and then began a three-year stint as a mature student. I thoroughly enjoyed myself on the course; my main subject was PE, of course, but I took maths as a subsidiary and found this both challenging and very satisfying. I was certainly at an advantage, having taught for so many years anyway, and I found the course quite easy. Living at home in Bromley with my wife and family, I would have to get up very early each morning to study and write all my essays. Of course I cycled in to college each day, and kept myself fit by working out in the college gym. After three years I came out as a fully qualified Cert. Ed., and in the first post that I acquired after qualifying, I quickly became acting Second of Department. I then went on to become Head of the Schools Sports Centre for the ILEA. The centre was in Morden, and was visited by pupils from all of the surrounding schools. A very rewarding job indeed, which enabled me to maintain the contact with the children, which I always enjoyed, but at the same time put into use my ability to organise and plan, and of course providing me with the opportunity to utilise all the sports which I had trained in.

In 1987, with the prospect of the ILEA being disbanded, I began to think about giving up teaching. I had not lost any of my enthusiasm for the job; I loved all the children and sport was still very important to me. But something had happened which had again altered the course of my life, and which made me think very seriously about what I wanted to be doing.

I was teaching at Catford Boys' School, at the time. In one of my classes I had a young boy who was always unwell. He was a bright, cheerful lad, but he would often look pale – sometimes almost blue about the lips. He was absent from school for long periods, as he suffered from heart disease and was being treated in hospital, where he would often be admitted for several days. He died, in the end, and was sadly missed by all those who knew him. I thought for a long time about this young lad, and how unfair it seemed that he should have suffered so much in his short life. Why was it that I had been blessed with good health, and the gift of physical fitness and strength, while others had to suffer illness and death? It seemed to me, as I pondered this question, that it was up to me to do something about it. I could no longer waste this gift I had, and I therefore began to think of ways I could help those who were less fortunate than myself.

I thought back to my days in the Middle East, when I had organised that charity walk across the desert for the war widows. Doing something that I thoroughly enjoyed, and at the same time helping others, seemed to me to be the most worthwhile way of spending time. Thinking about the little boy who had died, I decided that I wanted to help in some way. An organisation called STRUTH had been established, to support research into children's heart surgery at St Thomas's Hospital, in London. It was then, in 1987, that my plans to do something to raise money for this worthwhile cause began to take shape. Cycling was still the sport that I enjoyed the most, although, since I had started teaching full-time, I had not been out on my bicycle for over 25 years. Now I was planning to cycle from John O'Groats to Land's End – a distance of some 950 miles.

Chapter Four

John O'Groats to Land's End

STRUTH IS AN ORGANISATION that was set up in 1981 with the objective of raising money for the world renowned Heart Research Team based at St Thomas's Hospital. One of the projects being researched in 1988 was children's heart disease, and the preservation of the heart whilst undergoing surgery. If doctors could discover how to slow down the process of cell death in the heart whilst it was outside the body, then the urgency of heart operations would be far less and the risk of fatality greatly decreased. STRUTH were delighted that I was going to undertake a sponsored cycle ride for their cause, and I knew for sure that the money I raised was going to be well spent.

By this time, Olive and I had bought a little bungalow in the village of Kemsing, near Sevenoaks in Kent. It was a lovely spot for the children to grow up, away from the busy traffic and all the dangers and the dirt of South London. There are plenty of little winding narrow lanes bordered by deep hedgerows around the bungalow, which lead out into the heart of the Kent countryside. Gentle rolling hills, fields and woodland: it is a beautiful part of the country.

One Saturday morning, with the John O'Groats plan now firmly in my head, I went up into the loft where my old racing bike had been gathering dust over the years. I took it out into the garage and tested all the vital parts. A touch of oil here and there, the tyres pumped and a bit of a clean, and she was as good as new. I could feel the old excitement beginning to grow, as I said cheerio to the family and set off in the morning sunshine. I cycled ten miles that morning, and arrived back home feeling absolutely exhausted. Puffing and panting as I propped the bike up outside the house, I thought back to all those years of distance cycling and speed racing, and wondered how on earth I had ever managed it. The next day, though, I set out from home and cycled twenty miles, and did not feel nearly so bad at the end of it. The following day I added another ten. And so it built up, until I was managing a regular 250 miles a week. It was not long before I was once more beginning to feel as fit as I had done all those years ago. Cycling had once more become the most important thing in my life.

I planned the ride to take place over the school half-term holiday in May 1988, and I decided that, as well as raising money for research into heart surgery at St Thomas's, I would also use the trip for educational purposes. I was, at the time, the Kemsing "Grapevine" correspondent for Radio Kent, our local BBC station. This was a voluntary post, and involved scouting round for all the local news, views and events, and reporting them live, on the air. So it was quite easy for me to approach the Radio Station to ask for their support. They were very helpful indeed. I visited as many schools as possible in my local area, and found that the children were all extremely interested in the trip. It was arranged that they should follow my progress by listening in to Radio Kent each evening; they would not only be able to plot my journey, but I would also be able to ask them questions relating to my whereabouts which could then lead on to project work, either at primary or secondary level. Some of the work could even be incorporated into the CSE project work that the older children were doing at the time, and could be adapted for almost any subject – geography, history, even maths, for those who felt inclined to tackle the problem of gear ratios!

Since the days of the Tour of Britain and my winning streak up Shap Fell I had kept in touch with my old friend Jimmy Savile. His showbusiness career had of course gone from strength to strength, but his heart remained in the right place, and I knew his greatest concern still lay with helping others. He had, all along, been a great inspiration to me – and, I might add, he still is today. I decided to write to Jim and tell him about the trip I was planning and, true to form, he readily agreed to sponsor me. In fact, more than that, he also agreed to meet up with me, for old times' sake, at Shap Fell, as my route was to take me down the very same road. Unfortunately this never actually happened, as other events intervened for him, but as I was free-wheeling down that hill we had so valiantly struggled up together all that time ago, I couldn't help a smile appearing on my face!

I was hoping to raise £10,000 in all, and I was fortunate to have the backing of many local businesses, shops, community associations and individuals from the Sevenoaks area. The local community were absolutely marvellous. I was sponsored by local sports shops and associations, Hildenborough Cycles provided me with a bike, and Loxley's Garage also offered to supply a back-up vehicle, to be driven by our village policeman in Kemsing, PC Jim Panks. I thanked them very much for the offer but had to decline. No offence to Jim, but I was determined to do this trip alone. As the weather grew warmer I would spend my Saturday mornings outside Tesco's, in the High Street in Sevenoaks, pedalling away on a bicycle frame, which was supported on a specially adapted stand, whilst willing volunteers shook collecting buckets at passers by. I might have been travelling alone, but I knew I had the support and the goodwill of all the folks at home behind me. It is a marvellous feeling to be part of such an event which can unite the whole community.

By the beginning of May 1988 I seemed to have become something of a local celebrity, and I was kept extremely busy visiting various schools and other organisations to give talks. A week before I was due to leave, I was invited to crown pretty little Ciobhan Janetta as the May Queen at Seal Primary School spring fête. It was a lovely day, warm and sunny, and there was a

wonderful atmosphere, and again I was witness to the overwhelming generosity of ordinary folk.

At last the day of my departure dawned. I was to leave
Sevenoaks on Friday 27 May, to reach John O'Groats that evening, and planned to set off early Saturday on the first leg of the
trip. I was given a real hero's send off from Kemsing that day.
The local MP for Sevenoaks, Mark Wolfson, was there, as well
as several local dignitaries and councillors. Lancaster Jaguar (the
car firm) laid on a very grand reception and Nicola Wilmer, aged
9, was there to play the bagpipes, accompanied by her uncle,
Ronald Wilmer – and she made a delightful sound! All the local
primary schools were out in force, and the crowds cheered and
waved like mad as I cycled off in the warm May sunshine.

The train from London goes as far north as Wick. I had to
cycle from there up to John O'Groats, knowing full well I would
be cycling *back* down the very same road the following day. When
I arrived at my destination (or my starting point, if you like) I was
lucky enough to find a bed for the night. Of course, I hadn't booked
anything; I never do, but always assume that something will turn
up. Maybe I'm just very lucky, but I have never been disappointed
yet! I thought of all the advice I had received from various well-
wishers, the most recent being from some expert who told me on
no account should I *start* at John O'Groats, because of the pre-
vailing south-westerlies. I'm afraid always make a point of listening carefully to people's advice, and then doing exactly what
I like anyway! So here I was at John O'Groats, feeling as fit as a
fiddle, and ready for all the adventures that lay ahead.

The next day dawned bright and sunny, but bitterly cold. My
first task was to phone in to Radio Kent, to speak to all the
listeners of the Pat Marsh Show and this was the first of many
such telephone calls that punctuated the route. My plan to call
in regularly with details of my trip for all the school children
meant that I had to be near a phone between 6.00 and 7.00 p.m.
each evening. This was my only 'restriction' – I had no following

vehicle (again going against the advice of all the 'experts'!) and it was entirely up to me how far I travelled each day. Before I set off, I stood for a while on the rocks at John O'Groats, looking out to sea from the rugged coastline of northernmost Scotland. The lapwing and seagulls circled overhead, their raucous cry mocking me. "What a fool!" I could hear them shriek. But as I gazed out over the grey, choppy waters of the uninviting North Sea, I began to think about what lay beyond the horizon: Norway, the Arctic Circle, the Land of the Midnight Sun. Already my mind was laying plans for another trip, bigger and better and even more exciting than this first one ...

The first part of my journey took me straight down the A9, through Bonar Bridge, across the Moray Firth, to Inverness. This is a super road; it follows the coast all the way, the views are spectacular, and there is very little traffic indeed. It really was a marvellous feeling to be on my way at last, after all the preparation. Riding on a bicycle means you get to see so much more than when you are in a car; you have the time to appreciate all the detail of the landscape, and I must say that the scenery in Scotland was perhaps the most beautiful and the most impressive of the entire journey. It also gives you the freedom to stop and chat to people on the way – and my first memorable encounter of this trip was on the very first day when I saw a woman near the roadside wielding a heavy-looking spade and cutting what appeared to me to be squares of turf. I stopped, to take a drink from my water bottle, and we began talking. When I asked what she was about, she soon told me that she was in fact digging peat, to burn as fuel on her fire. I was intrigued, as I had never come across this before. I have smelt peat fires since, and can strongly recommend the use of this solid fuel – the sweet aroma from a peat fire must be one of the most warmly welcoming smells in the world. She was a lovely woman, with a gentle, lilting Scots accent, and the first of many interesting characters I was to meet along my way.

On my arrival in Inverness, I found a room for the night, and then had time to cycle on a little further, to the shores of Loch Ness itself. I had, of course, assured all the school children in Kent, all those miles away, that I would keep an eye out for the Loch Ness monster. I scanned the still waters of the Loch closely; it is such an enormous expanse of water that it is quite easy to understand how people believe that there may well be something lurking in its depths. What was that curious ripple out in the middle of the loch? I quickly found my camera, and took a shot. Then I investigated more closely with my binoculars. Alas. Two men in a rowing boat. I wonder how often they have been mistaken for a slimy, hump-backed, prehistoric creature?

After a good night's rest in Inverness, I set out once more at 8 o'clock on a fine May morning, ready for another day's hard cycling. The A9 continues south, through the Grampian Highlands, to the fine city of Perth. I felt that I was truly in the heart of Scotland now, with castles, mountains, forests, lochs and rivers seemingly in every direction. It was on this second day, however, that I had my worst disaster of the trip. Somehow the chain came off and became entangled in the wheel, loosening a couple of spokes. The bike began to wobble dangerously; I was all over the road and realised I would have to stop and sort out the problem. I was in quite an isolated part of the country, and couldn't for the life of me imagine being able to get to a repair shop for days. I thought the best plan would be to get to the nearest station and jump on a train to Glasgow, which according to the map seemed to be the only centre of civilisation and bicycle repair shops for miles. I managed to struggle the next 12 miles without a serious accident, and then arrived at the village of Speerbridge. Here I decided to seek out the police station – a tiny little house, where the village bobby was extremely helpful. He directed me to a chap in the village and told me just to knock at his front door. Full of misgivings, I followed his instructions, and was welcomed most sympathetically by a remarkable chap whose name, I regret to say, now escapes me. Having explained my predicament the chap gave my machine the once over, and then led me round the side of his house and down to the bottom of his garden, where stood a wooden shed. He opened the door of this shed and invited me to look inside. I could hardly believe my eyes, for the place was crammed to bursting with spare bicycle parts of every shape, size and dimension – enough, certainly, to have done any bike shop proud – and he proceeded to fix up my bike free of charge.

This was one of the many acts of kindness and consideration that endeared me to the Scots – never again shall I permit anyone to criticise them for being mean.

They are also blessed with a very sharp sense of humour, as was demonstrated to me that very evening. Despite the hold-up at Speerbridge, I covered over 100 miles that second day, and as the time drew near to make my phone-in to Radio Kent, I spied a modest-looking wayside inn, and decided to stop there and get a bite to eat. I walked in to a pleasant little bar/restaurant, with tables set for dinner and quiet music playing in the background. Behind the bar stood a small, ruddy-faced chap with a twinkle in his eye and a broad Scots accent. I looked at the menu he proffered, and when he asked what I wanted to order, I said that, as I was a visitor to Scotland, I had better try the haggis.

"Certainly, Sir," came the reply. "We have some fine haggis, but they are *extremely* fresh."

"That's fine by me," I replied. "The fresher the better!"

And with that my host left the bar, leaving the door to the back kitchen slightly ajar behind him. As I sipped quietly at my drink, taking in my peaceful surroundings, I was surprised to hear the noise of a shotgun going off. When the barman returned, he assured me my meal would not be long, and we proceeded to chat quite amicably about various subjects.

In about half an hour, a steaming hot plate of haggis appeared, together with the traditional mashed "neeps and tatties" (swede and potato). I ate the meal, which was extremely tasty, and then when I went up to the bar to pay my bill, was asked,

"Did you enjoy your meal, Sir?" and with that he solemnly presented me with a small feather.

"In fact, Sir, you may keep this as a memento of your visit. This belonged to your haggis, Sir, but it is a very rare thing. In Scotland we always use these to stuff our pillows, you see."

Of course I related this tale that evening on the telephone to the listeners of Radio Kent. Brian Faulkner, the host of the show, could not contain his amusement – he roared with laughter at the joke, but then added that of course, you must be sure never to eat the *legs* of the haggis!

From Perth, my route took me through Stirling, and then south of Glasgow and down the A74 to Carlisle. I managed to put in another 120 miles that day, and arrived that evening at Knutsford, near Warrington, having passed through Penrith, Windermere, Kendal and Preston. I now felt I had really broken the back of the trip, and was well into the swing of the ride. It is certainly an all-absorbing activity, and strange how it is possible for the mind to focus solely on the task in hand. As I rode steadily southwards, covering mile after mile, my mind was concentrating only on the riding. I think the rhythmical movement of the pedals, and the soothing sound of the wheels turning, helps in many ways to absorb all one's attention, but, apart from the intrusive noise of the passing traffic (and the stretch to Carlisle that day had been particularly busy!) I found there was very little to distract my mind from the cycling.

Again I managed to find somewhere to stay, just outside Knutsford. I had had to cycle on after stopping to make the Radio Kent call, so was fairly exhausted when I found somewhere at last – it must have been getting on for 8 or 9 o'clock in the evening. When I got talking with the proprietor of the small hotel and he found out what I was doing, he happily agreed to charge me only a nominal fee for my board that night.

The following day I made it down as far as Tewkesbury, a mere 95 miles, but I was battling against a strong headwind. Luckily the rain held off, but the wind always makes cycling much more difficult, and in some cases quite hazardous. At one point I was going past a stationary car, when the door opened suddenly, straight into the bike, and I was sent flying. The wheels skidded from under me, and I ended up in a tangled heap on the ground. I pulled myself up slowly, and managed to straighten out the bike. Luckily I was only bruised, but rather shaken, knowing that things could have been much worse. The driver of the car was very apologetic, and said that the wind had caught the door, but he didn't seem that bothered, and I tend to think that this was just one example of the carelessness and thoughtlessness of many British motorists. They just do not think, when it comes to cyclists, and I think much of the time they just don't *see* you, at all. I managed to straighten the handlebars of the bike, and get myself ready to set off again. I didn't say anything much, as I did not want to make a fuss, and after I had sorted myself out we shook hands and I continued on my way. However, such thoughtlessness was not confined to this incident alone, although this was perhaps the most serious. On more than one occasion I was knocked by an extending wing mirror on a car towing a caravan or trailer, which can produce a lovely bruise on your arm, and once I was hit by a coca-cola tin thrown from a car window. Often I had to swerve to avoid cigarette ends being carelessly thrown out of passing vehicles, again by people who just don't think, or bother to look where they are throwing things. It saddens me greatly, but I confess that by the end of the trip I came to expect that sort of inconsiderate behaviour.

A familiar sight in English lay-bys is the mobile café, or burger bar. I sped past many of these, the comforting and enticing smell of chips lingering for a long while in the air, and I often regretted not stopping. At some of them I *did* allow myself a rest, and really enjoyed a piping hot cup of tea and a good chat. The conversations I struck up beside these vans were some of the most memorable and enjoyable of the whole trip. At one, I recall, I was sharing the venue with a young chap who had a glider, transported on a trailer behind his vehicle. We got chatting, inevitably; he asked what I was up to and I explained, and then I questioned him about his chosen sport.

"Do you find a problem with low-flying aircraft?" I asked as a bit of a joke, imagining the possibility of meeting with an RAF fighter plane, or some such, to be very remote given today's stringent rules and regulations governing the airways. But he answered me in all seriousness, saying: "Well no, not really, but helicopters can be a problem."

I think, on reflection, I'll stick to the roadways. Coca-cola tins and cigarette ends are probably an acceptable risk given his alternatives!

The journey down through Britain was marked by the obvious difference in the scenery and surroundings, with dry stone walls giving way to tall hedgerows, and wide rolling fields taking the place of thick forests and mountains. Another noticeable difference throughout the country was the distinct accents I heard in each place I stopped. Even if I had not had a map with me, I'm sure it would always have been possible to pinpoint my location from the enormous variety of intonation I heard, whenever I stopped and got chatting. I suppose when you pass through so many different regions, the change in accents is particularly noticeable. From the dry lilting tones of the Yorkshireman, through the distinctive intonation and flat vowels of the Midlander, to the soft rounded lilt of the West Countryman, I came to appreciate the richness of the English language in all its colour and many different forms.

Throughout the whole of the trip, which lasted for just over one week, I was blessed with fine weather. Not that I object too much to the rain, but the wind can always be a problem, and certainly makes cycling much harder work.

The last leg of my journey was in many ways the most arduous. I was of course quite tired by this time, but I remember the final struggle from Penzance to Land's End seemed interminable. It was a really hard pull, and again I was battling against the wind. Every push on the pedals was an effort, and there were moments when I really thought my legs were going to seize up on me. However, the thought that I had all but achieved my goal was very encouraging, and I managed to concentrate hard on that fact. I was starving hungry, but determined not to stop before the end. And then I saw my first signpost to Land's End. What a marvellous feeling! Suddenly I forgot the aching pangs of hunger, and the pain in my legs. It was as if I had gained my second wind, and how exciting it was to see the miles gradually decrease on the signposts. Covering the last ten miles was wonderful. Tiredness and exhaustion gave way to a tremendous sense of excitement and fulfilment and I fairly flew that last stretch.

And now, the end was in sight. The sun had come out for my arrival at the final, southernmost tip of England, where the sea crashing on the rocks and sending up showers of spray, and the raucous seagulls calling overhead were both reminiscent of the place at the *other* end of Britain, where I had stood looking out to sea only eight and a half days before. I had cycled the entire length of Britain, covering 950 miles in all; I had seen some of the most beautiful scenery in the country, and I had met folk from all different walks of life, and from all different parts of Britain. Above all, I had raised £10,000 for research into heart surgery at St Thomas's Hospital, and I can tell you it was a marvellous feeling to have achieved this goal. As I climbed off the bike at last, my legs feeling just a little shaky from that final pull, I felt proud, and pleased and very, very satisfied. I could not help grinning from ear to ear as I signed the large book containing the signatures of all those who have made that same journey: and there are people arriving at Land's End from John O'Groats practically all the time. Some on foot, some on wheels – there is

Land's End at last!

quite an extraordinary collection, and it was a very proud moment when I added my name to the list and officially recorded my achievement.

I had arrived just thirty minutes ahead of schedule, but I was too early for my son, who was driving down from Kemsing to pick me up. I had to make my final phone-in to Radio Kent from Land's End, and Pat Marsh, whose show I was speaking on, relayed a message over the air to my son who was probably well out of range and somewhere in Cornwall: "Come on, hurry up – Dad's waiting for you!"

It was great to get home at last and put my feet up in a comfortable armchair, and have some good, home cooking. I didn't feel tired until about two or three days later, and fortunately the excitement kept me going until the following Wednesday, when a huge reception was laid on in Graham Webb's hairdresser's shop in Sevenoaks. Graham Webb had been one of the main sponsors for the trip, and crammed into his hairdresser's

With Nicola and Ronald Wilmer – a fine send-off ...

that evening were not only all my friends and family, but also
Mrs Sheila Cotton, the Deputy Sevenoaks Town mayor, and Mr
Colin Garner, vice-chairman of Sevenoaks District Council. Four
members of the Kemsing Singers had also formed themselves
(appropriately) into a barbershop quartet, and provided some

... and an equally rousing return. Kemsing Singers form a Barbershop Quartet, with Graham Webb (left) to welcome me home.

splendid singing as we were all wined and dined. The press were there, of course, and I was interviewed about the trip, and, although it is true that I felt quite elated, and a great sense of personal achievement, what still remained the most important thing for me, and what made it all worthwhile, was the knowledge that I had successfully raised money to help children undergoing heart surgery. Hopefully, in some small way, I had helped ease the pain and suffering and heartache of children and their families who are in such desperate need. For that reason alone, I think the trip had been successful.

My time was now taken up with answering all the many letters of congratulation and support that had arrived whilst I was away, and over the next few weeks. One of these, which I still have in my possession today, reads:

Well done Dave!

Best Wishes

Edwina Currie MP 15.6.88

I was asked to open school fêtes, and do the rounds of primary schools, WIs and other organisations, giving talks about my experiences. I thoroughly enjoyed myself doing this, and by now I was getting quite used to going down to the Radio Kent studios and giving live interviews on air. I felt that all the Radio Kent listeners, who had supported and encouraged me, were now like an extended group of friends.

Chapter Five

To the Arctic Circle

ONCE I HAD BEEN BACK AT HOME for a few months, and
had started teaching again, the excitement and publicity
surrounding the John O'Groats to Land's End ride
gradually died down. It was then, as the nights began to draw in,
and the winter months of 1988 provided plenty of long, dark
evenings with spare time to fill, that I began to plan for the next
adventure. I began to think of other trips I could make, and other
charities I could ride for. I kept thinking back to the time when
I was standing at John O'Groats, looking out at the cold, grey
waters of the North Sea. Norway: the land of fjords and the
Midnight Sun. I began to investigate. I looked at maps, and travel
brochures, and visited my local library to see if I could find out
more. The more I read, the more excited I grew; Norway
sounded a challenge, something different, but more than that, the
idea of reaching the Arctic Circle had now entered my head.
"Now there's a place!" I thought to myself. "Who has ever heard
of *anyone* cycling to the Arctic Circle?"

Once the idea had taken hold, I began to plan for the trip in
earnest. I spent many long hours poring over maps, trying to
decide upon a route. The starting point would have to be Oslo;
from there to the Arctic Circle did not look too difficult ... and
then my eyes strayed further up the map, to Lapland, to the
North Cape, the northernmost tip of Europe, and to Kirkenes,
on the Soviet border. Fired with enthusiasm I began my training
programme in earnest, and the winter months of 1988/89 passed
by with many long hours spent in the gym. Come the spring, my

routine consisted of arriving at the gym at 7.40 every morning, working with weights until 8.15 and, after a brisk shower, feeling quite ready for a day's teaching. I was cycling the 32 miles to London and back every day, as I was working at Forest Hill school in South London, at the time. With extra miles put in at weekends, this amounted to about 250 miles a week.

I also enrolled on an army survival course, which was held on Dartmoor over three days. This took place in January; it was cold, and misty, and the moor was probably at its most inhospitable. Having arrived at the centre where the course was based, I was shown a short film on survival technique, and then sent out with three soldiers to fend for myself on the moor. Although all three of my companions were survival experts, I was put in charge of the group, and made responsible for all decision making. It is true that the best way to learn is by doing something yourself, and it certainly helped me to remember exactly how to build and sustain a fire, catch rabbits, recognise edible leaves and mushrooms and other such useful tips. Much of the course was common sense, but it still helped to increase your awareness by actually doing something practical, rather than just reading up in a book. I was given information about food and nutrition, and told of the necessity of water – more important than food – for survival. Apart from being great fun the course also prepared me for any mishaps I might encounter whilst travelling alone in the harsh and isolated conditions of the Arctic Circle.

I had thought carefully about another suitable charity to ride for. I wanted to be able to help the people I knew, and to benefit the local community who had always been so supportive towards me. It was also the case that more and more high profile charities, many of which were based abroad, in the Third World, were taking all the money. Not that folk were any less generous, but the recession was beginning to bite, and the smaller, home-based charities were beginning to feel the pinch. *Hospice at Home*, a charity based in Tunbridge Wells, very quickly became the most obvious choice; I was aware of the dedication of the Hospice team, who help care for the terminally ill in the community, and knew only too well how anyone – including myself – might one day be in need of their services. Having decided upon a charity, I then began writing letters in earnest, to everyone I could think of – including the Prime Minister. I still have the letter which arrived on my doormat one day with "10 DOWNING STREET" at the top of the page, and which included the paragraph:

> The Prime Minister is impressed by your dedication and achievement in launching your venture and hopes you will convey her greetings and appreciation to the people and organisations in Norway who have so generously combined to support your venture.

I spoke to as many people as I could about my plans, and read everything I could lay my hands on. I wanted to be as fully prepared as possible, not only physically fit, but also prepared mentally for all the adventures that lay ahead. There was not a great amount of literature available. In my local library I found only three books on Norway, and information about Lapland was even more scarce. In one book I read which described their lifestyle, I learned all about reindeer stew, which has been the staple food of the Laplanders for hundreds of years. I imagined myself joining the Laps, perhaps travelling with them for a while, learning more about their lifestyle ... and possibly even getting to taste their legendary stew! I promised my old friends, the listeners of Radio Kent, that if I encountered anyone in Lapland, I would make sure that I would come back with the recipe for an authentic Laplanders' reindeer stew.

*   *   *   *   *   *

On 24 June 1989, just over one year after my return from the John O'Groats to Land's End trip, I set off once more, this time from Tunbridge Wells. My bike, worth £1,000, had generously been donated by Hildenborough Cycles. Specially adapted for the rigorous ride ahead, it had four carriers (front and back), fifteen gears in readiness for those steep mountain climbs ahead – and an excellent set of brakes! Also a little computer fitted to the front handlebar, which would be able to tell me how fast I was going, how many miles I had done, how many miles I still had ahead and the total mileage overall. This clever little gadget also told the time and had a stopwatch. It was to come in very useful indeed.

Crowds of people had once again gathered to see me off, many of them on bicycles themselves, and as I pedalled off on the road to Sevenoaks to the noise of wild cheering from the crowd, I was followed by a colourful group of supporters, all on a Fun Ride which was being sponsored to raise yet more money. It was certainly a moment to remember. In Sevenoaks the crowds had gathered too, and I was greeted by a rousing tune being played by the children of Kemsing Primary School. Local dignitaries – including the mayor – stood assembled in all their finery to greet me formally, and wish me well. I was given a letter from the mayor, Mrs Sheila Cotton, addressed to the mayor of Narvik, explaining who I was and what I was doing, and offering greet-ings and good wishes from the people of Sevenoaks to the people of Narvik. This I was entrusted to deliver by hand – and how proud I felt to be sent off on such an important errand.

From Sevenoaks I cycled to Heathrow Airport, from where I was due to take off the next day, 25 June, on a flight paid for by British Airways. I arrived in Oslo at 16.25 hours, and was greeted by one of my sponsors, who took me to a very fine hotel; I think it must have been one of the smartest in town. In the marble-tiled foyer, where fountains played and gentle music was piped, I had to wheel my bike through some very dignified-looking people. I have to say I felt rather uncomfortable, not being used to such grandeur, and I felt as if the smart set around me were all looking down their noses at this madman wheeling his bike around. Not the done thing in top class hotels, I'm sure. Still, this was an example of Norwegian hospitality, and also the fact that they were determined to treat me like a celebrity wherever I went. I think that even if I had been an official ambassador from England I could not have been given better treatment. I have to say that despite feeling somewhat misplaced, I did spend a most comfortable night in my luxury apartment. The next morning I was woken by a telephone ringing. I picked up the receiver and heard the familiar tones of Pat Marsh, from BBC Radio Kent, who wanted to interview me "live". It felt very strange to be talking to Pat from the comfort of a first-rate Norwegian hotel room – but also quite reassuring!

Thus sent on my way by the loyal and supportive listeners of my home county, my first port of call on the morning of 26 June was the City Hall. Cycling through the busy streets of Oslo I was struck by the cleanliness of this city compared to our own capital. The City Hall itself overlooks Oslofjord – the main shipping thoroughfare, linking the city to the rest of the world via the sea. Boats, ships, yachts, windsurfers – watercraft of all shapes, sizes and colours bob up and down at the head of the most important fjord in Norway, and directly in front of the city's commercial centre. Here, on the steps of the City Hall, I had to confront the television cameras – my meeting with the mayor was to be broadcast nationwide. This media attention was something I was to get used to – throughout the entire trip I was given excellent coverage, not just locally, as at home, but nationally. Apparently I became known throughout the whole of Norway as that "nice eccentric Englishman". The national newspapers covered my trip, and on one occasion I appeared as front-page news. So, in front of the TV cameras and radio mikes, the Mayor presented me with a book about Oslo and a donation for the Hospice, and wished me well.

Then I was off – weaving my way through the morning

rush-hour traffic of Oslo and negotiating the unfamiliar tram lines. These latter really gave me the feeling that I was in a foreign place, and certainly took some getting used to. They can prove hazardous for bicycle wheels! Once I had left behind the hubbub and the dust of the city I began to make very good time. The countryside around Oslo is reasonably flat; the roads are wide and smooth and there are excellent cycle paths, where the old roads have been maintained after motorway development – very wide, and well-kept, and a marvellous asset to the cyclist. I sped along with the wind on my back, feeling the familiar exhilaration that I always experience when starting out on a trip. The air was clear and fresh, and the countryside seemed to stretch on for miles and miles. The sky was a dazzling, deep blue, and the fields looked remarkably lush and green. The houses are often painted a brilliant white, with startling red roofs, and everywhere looks extremely neat, tidy and clean. It is a wonderful sight to see the open road stretching before you, and to feel the miles slip by with the power of the pedals. Mountains began to appear on the distant horizon – abrupt ridges leading on from peak to peak as far as the eye could see, and I could feel my excitement increase with the knowledge that before long I would be amongst those very mountains, snow-capped, beautiful and isolated.

My first adventure befell me on that very first day. I had cycled about 80 miles – it had been an easy ride but I had finished all the water that I was carrying in my two water bottles. It was then that I saw a gentleman watering his garden with a hosepipe. I stopped and asked him (in English and sign language) if I could fill my bottles. I also asked if he knew of anywhere that I could camp for the night. He seemed to recognise me – I gathered later that he had seen me on the television – and in broken English and his own sign language he eagerly indicated that he wished me to stay *there* for the night. I assumed that he was offering his front lawn as a camp site – it was as smooth and as neat as a bowling green – but I was ushered into the house from where he telephoned his daughter, who lived on the neighbouring farm. She arrived, and happily spoke perfect English, so was able to explain that I was being offered a bed for the night. I was entertained royally that evening, and given my first taste not only of Norwegian cuisine, but also the hospitality and friendliness which is so typical of the country. I slept soundly in a large, soft

Asa and Ole Kristensen – my hosts in Norway.

comfortable bed, and awoke feeling refreshed and eager to cover more miles. Just as I had finished eating a hearty breakfast, however, and was preparing to say my farewells and get on my way, the lady of the house ushered in two reporters. From two rival newspapers, they were both keen for my story, and so the first hour of day 2 was spent speaking to them and yet again having my photograph taken. My kindly hosts were trying to persuade me to stay another night, but I was now keen to press on, and so bade them farewell. Before I left, they telephoned their other daughter, who lived two days' ride away, and provided me with another address for the night. They were evidently delighted to have had the opportunity of enteraining me, and wished me well enthusiastically. I felt deeply touched by their kindness and generosity.

In these first few days of the ride I covered about 90–100 miles a day quite easily. The roads were on the whole well-maintained, the weather was good, and the scenery was beautiful. I felt grateful for all those hours spent in the gym, and the cycle rides to and from London, which meant that I now felt extremely fit, and was able to cover the miles with considerable ease, and plenty of enjoyment. At all times along the route I was most impressed with the friendliness and openness of the people I met; I never once felt a stranger, and was often recognised. I recall one time when I had stopped at the roadside, and was approached by a gentleman with a very recognisable accent who asked without any introduction, "Are you the Englishman?"

"I don't know if I am *the* Englishman," I replied, "but I certainly am *an* Englishman."

We struck up conversation, and it transpired that he, too, was English but had sold up his house and together with his wife was travelling around the world in his caravanette. They were a lovely couple, and welcomed me in to their small home on wheels, where I shared a cup of tea and many interesting stories. Before I left they gave me a £50 donation for the Hospice, which was most gratefully received.

By the time I reached the outskirts of Trondheim, on 29 June, I was making such good time that I was able to make a short detour, and avoid the heavy, noisy traffic. I was reluctant to have to face the hustle and bustle of a busy city after the peace and quiet of the countryside. What is most memorable about the countryside in Norway is the vast sense of space – so different from the narrow lanes and hedgerows of the south of England. To me it felt like the difference between the space in a broom cupboard and a medieval castle. Fields and forests seem to stretch endlessly, horizons uninterrupted by buildings, and vast expanses of open sky above. The deep silence is penetrating; there are so few cars on the roads, even on the main route that I was following.

From Trondheim to Kirkenes is 1,250 miles. I knew that I had covered the easiest part of the journey so far, and the real challenge still lay ahead. The weather, which had up until now been clean and fine, now took a turn for the worse. A side wind was buffeting the bike, and at times I was forced to get off and push. At one point I remember I had to cross a bridge, and found this particularly hard; the wind was so strong that I had to fight to keep the bike steady, and found that I had to turn my head to one side in order to breathe. It was while I was struggling in this wind that I stopped at a cafeteria by the side of the road. There are many of these in Norway – usually log cabins which are always warm and welcoming inside. I went in, grateful to get out of the wind for a bit, and was greeted with the delicious smells of coffee and hot food. On the menu I was very excited to read that Reindeer Stew was on offer. Of course I could not resist ordering, having read so much about the dish. A steaming hot bowl soon arrived, and I can assure you that it was one of the most delicious meals I have had in my life. A very tasty, and heart-warming stew, with absolutely no fat in it whatsoever. No wonder the Laps, who are supposed to survive on the stuff, have a very low incidence of heart disease!

The countryside was beginning to change – becoming much

more mountainous as I approached the Arctic Circle. One mountain I remember with clarity: as I started to climb, dark rain clouds began to appear, and a light drizzle was falling steadily. I pushed on, up an up, each hairpin bend bringing me slightly nearer the summit. By the time I had reached the top of the mountain I was soaked to the skin, but there was absolutely no point in stopping as the clouds hung low over the mountain top and there seemed to be no chance of the rain letting up. So I decided to keep going, and began the descent – as always a fairly steep, winding road with a sharp drop on one side. The rain stopped at last, and with the wind whistling though me I could begin to feel myself drying out. The sun came out too, and ahead of me, on the road, I could see a herd of reindeer – always a spectacular and thrilling sight. The bike sped down the mountain, and, as I felt the speed gathering, I decided to glance at the computer on the front handlebar which could tell me how fast I was going. I was slightly perturbed when I discovered that I was doing 35.5 m.p.h! Realising that this was a little too fast, even for drying-out purposes, I applied the brakes to slow myself down. I then heard the noise that every cyclist dreads – the distinctive snap of the front brake cable. Realising that a crash was inevitable, I quickly unclipped my toe straps in preparation for an emergency escape. The herd of reindeer, which I had admired from afar, now loomed closer and closer; they were ambling slowly across the road and I was willing them to quicken their pace, but it was too late; yelling at the top of my voice to the slow, ambling beasts to get out of my way, I attempted to steer but my bike was out of control and I caught the rear end of one of the animals at a speed of about 20 m.p.h. The bike shot into the air and a sensation roughly equivalent to 250 volts lifted me off the saddle. I landed with a bump at the side of the track, luckily a fairly soft verge, and lifted my head to see the bicycle continue to career down the mountainside. Finally it stuttered to a halt, and lay, like me, in a fairly forlorn heap somewhat further down the road, wheels spinning and handlebars in the air. I just sat for a while, gathering my wits. I realised I had not been badly hurt, and as I gazed up at the now clear blue sky above me, I just felt immensely grateful, knowing full well that the accident could have been far worse. I finally got to my feet and began to walk rather shakily down the track towards my bicycle. I could see the reindeer I had hit, still standing at the side of the track – *he* certainly did not seem any the worse for wear, but just wore a faintly bemused expression. When I reached the bike I could see at once that the handlebars had become twisted, and two of the pannier bags were entangled in the wheel spokes, but apart from that my trusty machine had sustained little injury. One and a half hours later and I had sorted out all the problems, and was on my way once more. Incidentally, I must say that one of the saddest sights in Norway was the number of reindeer you see at the side of the road that have been hit by cars. Far worse than the rabbits we often see in this country.

It was after this little escapade that I had to face one of the hardest challenges of the ride: from Mo i Rana, an old mining town at the head of Eisfjord, the road wends its way inland, and up into the mountains of Salt Fjellet. I was following the E6 (European route 6), which is the main road running the entire length of the country. There is, incidentally, only the one major road, with a few minor roads leading off west to the coast and east to the Swedish border. As I pressed on northwards, and eastwards, the road grew steeper and steeper. The terrain changed quickly and noticeably, from pastureland, to thickly forested hillsides, to bare, rocky outcrops. The mountains here are all well over 1,500 metres. As I cycled up the gradual incline at the start of the ascent, the mountains loomed way up above me. Looking up, the peak ahead of me seemed to go on and on – I could not imagine ever reaching the top. Ahead, in the gentle foothills, small wooden houses nestled in the trees, smoke rising in silent columns from their chimneys; I shall always remember that

A roadside cabin in Norway.

Not only cars use the highway.

pungent smell of woodsmoke mingling with the sweet scent of the pine trees in the clear, sharp air. The scenery here was truly breathtaking; herds of graceful reindeer nibbled peacefully in the stretches of grassland between the outcrops of rock, and birds swooped overhead, filling the air with their song. As I gradually climbed, I could feel the cold air beginning to bite. For the first time I had to delve into my carriers for my warm gloves and an extra pullover. I had my first sighting of an elk on this climb; an impressive beast, huge, lumbering and powerful. Still the mountain top loomed overhead, its snow-topped peak looking quite threatening against the dark grey sky. The road continued to rise gradually, wending its way round and round. I was able to keep riding, slipping up the gears as the incline increased. I suddenly noticed that I had left the trees behind; the landscape changed, and became more bare and rocky. Snow appeared at the side of the road, which I could now see was covered in ice. With my head bent down, and my legs pushing steadily on the pedals, I noticed a film of ice beginning to form on the handlebars, with tiny little icicles hanging off the brake cables. I was determined to keep going, but was beginning to feel the pain of the hard climb; the wind was penetrating and my eyes were not focussing properly. I stopped to rest, and have a drink – unfortunately I only had a cold drink with me – but it was enough to refresh me. Rummaging in my panniers I retrieved an old newspaper which I stuffed up the front of my pullover for a bit more insulation. I then climbed back on to to the bike, determined now to make the top in one go. The snow was quite thick on the ground now, and I could feel the wheels slipping on the ice-covered road, but the sun was trying hard to break through the cloud; as I rounded the final bend I could hardly contain my feeling of joy as I saw the large sign: "THE ARCTIC CIRCLE". I jumped off the bike and just lay down in the snow, utterly exhausted but exhilarated too. I had been looking forward to this moment for so long; all those months of planning and studying maps over the kitchen table at

At the Arctic Circle.

home – and now here I was at last. Thoughts of home led me to recall that the south of England was at this moment suffering a heatwave – a thought which certainly brought a smile to my face as I lay there in the deep snow of the Arctic Circle!

I can't remember how long I lay there, getting my breath back and relaxing my aching muscles, but I gradually became aware of how cold and damp and uncomfortable I was feeling. I lifted myself up and looked about properly for the first time, and the sight which met my eyes made me catch my breath. The view was truly spectacular; an icy, barren space with no visible life apart from the reindeer and elk I could see in the distance. It was an astonishing sight; inhospitable and threatening and quite awesome.

Just to the side of the road was the welcoming sight of a log cabin, smoke rising from the chimney pot, and cars pulled up outside – obviously belonging to the tourists who had come up the easy way! Inside I was greeted by the warmth of a roaring log fire, and the enticing smell of hot coffee. I was, of course, the only cyclist to be visiting the place, and quickly engaged in conversation with the folk inside. I sat by the fire in my wet clothes, steam rising from my damp pullover, and drank mug after mug of delicious hot coffee. A German couple struck up conversation with me, and once I had got dry they invited me to join them for some hot soup. It turned out they were visiting the place on their honeymoon – quite an unusual destination, I thought, although I think they thought that what *I* was doing was even more unusual.

It was possible to buy a certificate here, which I still treasure to this day, which gives me the "Freedom of the Arctic Circle with all the rights and privileges thereto pertaining, to henceforth enjoy without let or hindrance." This impressive document continues:

His Majesty Jack Frost, King of the Arctic, Emperor of Blizzards and Lord of a million snowflakes, hereby declares that the crossing was made this 3rd day of the month of July in the year 1989.

Asking where I might stay for the night, I was directed to a small hotel – one of the many roadside log cabins funded by the local council – where I had a good night's sleep. I awoke the following morning feeling bright, fit and quite ready for another day's long ride. I must say that all those long hours of training paid off; I have always been grateful for the fact that, no matter how exhausted I might feel at the end of a day's ride, a good night's sleep will put me to rights and I always wake up feeling completely refreshed and ready to start again.

Chapter Six

Beyond the Arctic Circle – a trip to the Border

A S I SET OUT to continue my journey northwards, I lost
the height I had gained the previous day. I left behind the
ice and snow and barren rock of the mountain top; the
sun came out and my spirits began to rise as I rode slowly and
carefully down the steep road, which had a sheer drop on one
side. Gradually I emerged into a different world, with gently
rolling grassland and an area carpeted with the most rich and
colourful display of wild flowers I have ever seen. I could not
begin to name them, there were so many different varieties, but
I had to stop and get my camera out to record this astonishing
sight for all the people at home. I had certainly not expected such
abundant wildlife north of the Arctic Circle; as well as all the
flowers I can also remember all the many birds singing in the
clear air. I am sure that all the tourists who visit the place in their
cars never really appreciate its full beauty and richness – it is
always possible to see, hear and smell so much more on a bicycle,
and actually feel a part of the countryside you are exploring. It
is quite a different experience from motoring though anywhere,
and in my opinion it is possible to gain so much more.

I was now on my way to Narvik, following the E6 which runs
parallel to the coastline. Famous for its beautiful, indented fjords
Norway's coast provides some spectacular views – a remarkable
legacy from the Ice Age – with the white, snow-capped peaks of
the mountains providing a stunning backdrop to the clear, still

waters of the wide, deep fjords. Memories of Loch Ness paled in comparison to these wonderful sights. Instead of the road following the contours of these fjords, there used to be several ferry crossings, to simplify the journey. More recently, however, long tunnels have been built to make the journey quicker, and only one ferry remains. Fine if you are in a car, but now I was at a disadvantage on my bicycle. I did not relish the thought of long, dark, damp tunnels, and became increasingly worried at the prospect as I approached the first. I was then to discover that a special bus was provided for anyone on foot or on two wheels. I decided, with a certain relief, to make use of the facility, and I have to say I felt really quite thankful to be able to hand my bike over to the officials who quickly attached it to a special carrier on the back of the bus. I climbed on board, and sat back to relax in my seat. It felt very strange to see the scenery speed by so quickly, but I was very glad as we entered the darkness of the first tunnel. Seven tunnels in all, and they seemed to go on for ever. Letting the bus take the strain gave me a fine opportunity to have a rest, take stock of my trip so far and think carefully about what lay ahead.

My next destination was Narvik, 210 km north of the Arctic Circle and situated on Ofot Fjord. After the final tunnel, the road wends its way along the side of the fjord; it was evening, and yet the sun was still high in the sky, and the daylight showed no signs of dwindling. As far as I was concerned, it could well have been 11 o'clock in the morning. The waters of the fjord glinted in brilliant sunlight, their still depths reflecting with mirror-like accuracy the peaks of the mountains behind.

Narvik was the site of the first allied victory in Norway in World War II – the famous Battle of Narvik in 1940. The town was almost completely flattened by bombing, and has been largely rebuilt since the war. Angular modern buildings grace wide, treeless streets; the air is crisp and sharp and there is an aura of cleanliness about the place. My first task, as always, was to find a place to sleep, and then to eat before settling down for the night. I stayed in a modern, but relatively cheap, hotel, where the service, as always, was efficient and the warmth of the hotelier characteristic of all Norwegians I had met so far. It felt strange to shut the curtains on a world that was still in brilliant sunshine, but it was 11 o'clock at night, and I was weary after a long day's haul.

The following morning it was as bright at 7.00 a.m. as it had been when I finally got to sleep the night before. My first mission was to make my way to the City Hall to meet the mayor, and present him with the letter from Mrs Cotton that I had carried all the way from Sevenoaks. I cycled through the wide, clean streets, the main thoroughfare lined with modern grey-roofed buildings and shops leading towards the eight-storey-high tower block of the Town Hall. Fountains play in the square in front of the building, and the statue of Liberation – an impressive monument of a mother and child – is the focal point of the square. Within the graceful, polished entrance hall, the media were once again in evidence: this was indeed a great occasion for the people of Narvik. I was welcomed by the mayor, Mr Anduassion, and ushered in to a parlour where I was given coffee and cakes. We chatted together for some time: like so many of the Norwegians I met, he was at once warm, friendly and welcoming. We discovered that we shared the same profession – he, too, was a teacher, and had been the headmaster of a local school. He informed me that, despite being appointed as Mayor for a three-year period he was still being paid a full salary as a teacher. He showed me around the Town Hall, with its polished granite, plate glass and wood. We returned to the parlour for more coffee, from where I was due to give a radio interview, on BBC Radio Kent, with my old friend Pat Marsh. I had, in fact, been reporting regularly to the listeners back home, and I know that many school children had been plotting my route. Mr Anduassion was very nervous at the prospect, as he had never spoken on the radio before. I reassured him, and told him to imagine that he was just speaking to an individual and having an ordinary conversation. We both spoke on the telephone to Pat Marsh; I spoke first, telling the listeners my most recent news, and then Mr Anduassion took the receiver, and in his heavy Norwegian accent sent greetings and friendship to all in Kent from the people of Narvik. After the event he looked extremely pleased with himself! He handed me a book before I left, with the inscription inside:

> In remembrance of an interesting talk and special experience. G. Anduassion, 7.7.89.

During the war, the Royal Engineers First Division had sustained tragic heavy losses in Narvik after their attempt to destroy a German plant manufacturing hard water – a component of atomic bombs. Bad weather conditions had resulted in their plane flying off course and crashing in the mountains. I had been asked by many people living in the Kent area if I would visit the War Graves in Narvik, to see if I could trace the memorials of any of their missing relatives. I found the Cemetery, just outside the city. It was a very peaceful place, nestling in the pine-forested foothills of the mountains that cradle the city, and I was impressed at how neatly and immaculately it was maintained. Tucked away in the corner of the cemetery was a beautiful little chapel, which I entered; it was certainly very peaceful there, and a memory I shall cherish. I looked carefully amongst the graves for any indication of servicemen related to the people I knew in Kent, but to no avail. I felt disappointed that I would not be able to return with any news, but knew that I had done my best.

Although it was very interesting to stop in Narvik and speak to the people, I was eager, as always, to get going again. My first major achievement in Norway had been to reach the Arctic Circle; the goal that lay before me now was the North Cape, another almost legendary place, famous for its location on the northernmost tip of Europe – the point at which Europe meets the Arctic Ocean. I recall standing on the rocks of John O'Groats and thinking about what lay beyond the waters of the

North Sea. Now I was looking forward to standing on the rocks
of the North Cape and thinking of what lay beyond the Arctic;
there is no more land between the North Cape and the North
Pole.

North of Narvik, the road deteriorated noticeably. Although
the roads further south are all in excellent condition, they were
now, in the north of the country, to prove unpredictable. Often
the firm tarmac would give way to a mixture of rock and gravel
up to 4 inches deep in places, and the road would also be full of
potholes for several miles – certainly not conducive to safe and
easy cycling. Apart from substantially slowing down my progress, I was worried that these conditions would cause undue
wear and tear on the bike – although I have to say I very rarely
worried about my *own* safety. However, although the roads may
have worsened, the weather began to improve. The sun came out
… and *stayed* out. I was now well and truly in the magical Land
of the Midnight Sun, where it is daylight for twenty-four hours.
There is continuous daylight for 73 days and nights of the year
in this part of the country; children play football at 1 o'clock in
the morning, and the birds never stop singing. The sun actually
traverses the sky, but on touching the horizon rises instantly
again. For most of the time it is overhead, and there is no indication, according to the quality of the light, as to the time of day.
I have to say I was completely confused; one evening I kept on
cycling until the early hours of the morning. Looking at my
watch only increased my sense of bewilderment – I really could
not tell whether it was 2 o'clock in the morning or 2 o'clock in
the afternoon! I quickly became quite exhausted, with my regular
sleep patterns disturbed and my sense of time quite disorientated.

Before reaching the North Cape, I had to negotiate a three-
mile-long tunnel – no bus this time, so there was nothing for it
but to plunge into the cold darkness. Inside the tunnel, water was
pouring from the roof for the full length, and as I cycled quickly
through I remember feeling quite anxious, wondering what else

might be about to fall from above me. Pedalling along with my mind thus preoccupied, and feeling increasingly wet and uncomfortable with all the water pouring down over me, I suddenly became aware of a movement up ahead. Braking quickly, I swerved to slow down just in time – imagine my surprise when I saw a herd of about twenty reindeer emerging from the gloom and walking slowly in my direction. They trotted past me, quite unaware of such an unusual intruder in their tunnel – all looking as if they owned the place and ignoring me completely.

By the time I reached the end of the tunnel I was absolutely soaked to the skin. It was a great relief to see daylight again, and the sun was still shining brilliantly, so I dried off in no time. My next port of call was the town of Alta, and this journey took me through some of the most wild and rugged terrain I have ever seen. The deep and penetrating silence all around me, broken only by the regular, rhythmic turning of my bicycle wheels,

An entrance to one of the many tunnels on the E6.

En route in the Land of the Midnight Sun

added to the sense of remoteness and isolation. I cycled up mountains without stopping, arriving at the top feeling breathless and
exhilarated. The views were spectacular, and I think I had every
right to feel "on top of the world".

From Alta, the road continues northwards, and then ends
abruptly at Kafjord, about thirty miles south of the North Cape.
Those in coaches, cars or on bicycles have to take a 45-minute
ferry crossing to Honningsvag, the main town on the island
which is right off the northernmost tip of Norway. Getting off
the ferry, I decided to set up my tent for the night, and then leave
my luggage here and cycle the rest of the way. The North Cape
was the name given to the majestic cliffs which form the final
bastion against the menacing waters of the Arctic Ocean. These
rocks were apparently named in 1553 by the Englishman Richard
Chancellor on his search for the north-east passage to China.

There are many facilities for tourists here, with the opportunity to buy gifts and souvenirs, and plenty of craftware made by the Laps, or Sami, as they prefer to be called. I was looking forward to seeing some of these crafts first-hand, rather than displayed on the counter of a tourist gift-shop.

After leaving the North Cape I headed for Karasjok, which is about a hundred miles south. This journey took me along a road which hugged the coastline as far as Lakselv, and then heads inland for some fifty miles. The roads were now very poor – some of the worst I have ever experienced. I also felt far more isolated than I have ever done before. I am sure this began to affect my mind – I remember on one occasion I was convinced that a bird was following me, and I began talking to it: "What are you doing here? Why are you following me?"

I have always loved being out on my own, cycling along deserted roads. My training for any major ride has always started first thing in the morning, when you can feel the freshness of the dew in the air, and see the leaves and the grass glittering in the pale early light. I love cycling through the quiet country lanes of Kent, where pheasants, rabbits and the occasional badger roam freely. Cottages half-hidden behind trees and deep foliage still have their curtains tightly drawn against the world, and there is a great sense of privilege at being able to share this time with nature. As I take in the peacefulness of the gentle rolling hills I always think how fortunate I am – I would not in a million years swap places with the busy commuter who would be gliding through these lanes in his car in an hour or so. The quality of loneliness in this wild and rugged Scandinavian land was quite different, however, from the special feeling of peace in an English country lane. Although it was beautiful, this was, too, a vast and inhospitable land, where the silence and isolation were at times quite threatening. It was especially so at night, I recall, when the feeling used to become quite physical; almost like a sharp ache, and a yearning for someone to talk to, combined with the gnawing uncertainty I felt before I had found a place to camp for the night. However, once I had found a suitable spot, and crawled into my tent, I always found it easy to relax and let the worries of the day fade away. Waking up in the morning, fully refreshed and ready for the next leg of the journey would always renew my excitement and sense of adventure. Whom would I meet? What would I see? I knew that something exciting always lay around the next corner … After a habitual breakfast of bread, cheese and sardines I would pack up the panniers again, brush any snow and ice off the bike, and set off once more, feeling at one with with nature and drinking in the deep quiet of the hills and mountains, forests and rivers.

Lapland covers the northernmost part of Scandinavia and Russia. Crossing the borders between the Scandinavian countries in these parts is no problem at all; I knew that towards Kirkenes I might have some difficulty, though, as it is on the border of the former Soviet Union and lies in what is described as a 'sensitive' area. Meanwhile I was to experience the warmth and friendliness of the Sami, and visit towns of Tana and Karasjok, which both lie in the heart of Lapland.

I was lucky enough to have an opportunity to speaking to the Sami; throughout my entire trip I had found the Scandinavian people warm, friendly and welcoming, and the Sami were certainly no exception. Cycling along a deserted road one day, I came across a very colourful sight: a camp of bright, circular tents – rather like the Indian tepees – some with columns of smoke rising from a hole in the top. Stools were set up in front of the camp, with reindeer hides stretched out on them, and several artefacts made from the hide set out too. I assumed these were for sale, but could not imagine that there was much passing trade in this remote and deserted area. The few people I had seen about were all local Norwegians anyway; there certainly did not seem to be any tourists anywhere. I stopped and got off the bike, and wandered over to where the goods were displayed. As always, I soon got into conversation, although I had to rely quite heavily on international sign language this time. I managed to find out, however, that the artefacts were only being prepared here, and that they would be taken to sell in the west, at various places on the coast, where the majority of Norwegians actually live and where the tourist trade is busiest. I explained as best I could what I was doing; I showed them my bicycle, and my map, pointing out all the places I had been.

"You are a traveller too!" was the exclamation, and with the realisation that I was "one of them" I was welcomed into their camp, and invited to share some food. As well as their colourful tents, they also had one or two caravans. I showed them my own small tent, and was directed to a space where I could put it up. This done, I was invited to join a group who were sitting around a large log fire. At another fire nearby, some women were busy preparing food. I asked what was in their pot.

"Stew," came the reply. I knew only too well that this could mean only one type of stew.

A very large, old, iron pot hung over the fire, and it seemed to be filled to the brim with water, which bubbled over the top and hissed and spluttered onto the logs of the fire. It looked to me as if it was too full, but I watched quietly as preparations continued. One woman was bent over a table, chopping the hind leg of a reindeer – recognisable by its size and shape. She hacked away at this, and then threw all the pieces roughly into the pot. A few minutes later a small boy appeared, carrying an armful of what looked like tree leaves. I have no idea at all what sort of leaves they might have been, but they all went into the pot too. A large white cod, minus head, was the next item to be thrown in to the bubbling mixture, and finally several handfuls of wild mushrooms, which grow in abundance in these parts. We sat pleasantly chatting and laughing until the meal was prepared; when it came, I was presented with a huge bowl – more the size of a washing up bowl than anything else – and the Sami people

Sami tents on the roadside.

Selling their wares.

grinned as I tasted my first mouthful. It was delicious! A taste I shall never forget, and like the stew I had tasted in the restaurant before, it was again extremely lean. I was told that this is why only the hind leg is used for the stew, although every other part of the reindeer is used in some way, too. After a long chat around the fire, I crawled at last into my tent. I felt extremely safe and secure that night, listening to the sounds of these people who spend their lives travelling and sleeping in the open, and I slept very soundly indeed. The next day was bright and sunny; I packed up my things, and wheeled my bike onto the road, ready to depart. The whole camp had gathered to see me off, and there were tears in their eyes as we said our farewells. I was so impressed with the genuine warmth and friendliness of these most unusual people, and felt extremely lucky to have been able to spend some time with them.

I was to see many more Sami camps on my travels around Lapland; the travellers would always stand at the roadside, smiling and waving as I passed by. I think that it was such an unusual sight for them – I only ever saw about three or four other cyclists throughout my entire trip in Norway – and of course I was still receiving a lot of publicity in the Norwegian press. When I reached Tana, a small town on the Tana River just north of Finland, I was greeted by the 'Sami Radio Company', Finmark Daily, and also a delightful group of people from Tana's 'Culture Centre'. Here I also met the Director of Education, who had been informed of my visit. I had brought with me a small parcel of photographs and work from the children of Kemsing Primary School, in the hope that they might be able to correspond with the children from Tana. Although there are three main languages here (Norwegian, Finnish and Lappish) many of the people speak English. The Director of Education said he was honoured to be able to greet me, and once more I was made to feel very welcome, and quite a celebrity.

Cycling in the vast open spaces in this far northern land, I often grew quite exhausted. One or two incidents I recall are typical of the time:

On one occasion, when I had been cycling steadily for about fifty miles, I began to feel tired and rather hungry. Realising I would have to stop and eat before I could go on much further, I slowed down and jumped off the bike, sitting down on the soft verge at the side of the track. It was very, very quiet – a deep silence that seems far more still and undisturbed than anything I know in England. In the distance I could see reindeer and Sami farmers – the only sign of life. The hills and the forests just seem to stretch endlessly in all directions. I searched through my bags to try and find something to eat, and came up with a half-finished loaf which must have been in my bag for about three days, and a tin of sardines. Alas! no tin opener in evidence! My pen-knife had a tin opener attachment ... but where was that pen knife? It's always the same, whenever I need anything. I searched through every single bag, and of course, found the pen knife, triumphantly, in the bottom of the very last bag. My stomach was complaining loudly by now, and I opened the tin carefully, ready to partake of this sumptuous feast. All of a sudden, as if from nowhere, the air around me was filled with a dark cloud of mosquitoes. I could not believe how large the little monsters were, and they were dive-bombing from all sides. I grabbed my mosquito net and sat with it over my head – unable to partake of my meal until the noisy brutes lost interest and disappeared. My can of mosquito repellant was certainly one of the most useful items that I took with me on the trip! The rain usually kept them at bay, and I was often grateful for the intermittent showers, but they really were the most unpleasant hazard.

Another time when I was quite overcome with exhaustion was on the road to Karasjok. I had been cycling for some time without seeing anybody at all, and gradually began to recognise the symptoms of extreme tiredness. I stopped at frequent intervals to drink from my water bottle, but knew that I would have to

stop finally for the night before long. I did not even think that I
had the energy to put the tent up. As I continued to push on the
pedals, I felt a giddy sensation, and my eyes would not focus
properly. It was a relief when I reached the brow of a hill and
could free-wheel down. And then, ahead of me at the side of the
road, I saw a small, low-lying wooden building and, to my immense relief, the word "HOTEL". I could not have cared how
much this was going to cost me; I propped the bike up outside
and wandered, unsteadily, into the warm, clean interior. It turned
out that the place had only been built six months previously, and
was an expensive place to stay, but I ordered some food, and a
bed for the night, and, of course, got talking. The proprietor
knew exactly who I was and what I was doing; he had seen my
picture in several newspapers, and even knew that I was in the
area. When it came to settling the bill in the morning he cheer-
fully knocked £10 off the price, and urged me to come back for
another visit soon!

My nightly lodgings varied considerably throughout the trip.
This added another dimension to the whole experience, and each
stop contributed in some way to the richness of the ride. I recall
stopping at one house that had rooms to let, where the people
were extremely friendly but seemed to live in a certain amount
of chaos. In order to reach my room I had to climb over piles
of timber and old pipes, and when at last I got to the room I
discovered a pile of tools heaped up in the shower cubicle!
Most of the time I camped in my familiar little tent, which
became like a second home to me. I stayed on mountains or in
woods, miles from the nearest human being, but close to nature and not at all far from various wild animals, which would
often wake me at night. Possibly the most hair-raising event
was when I was sound asleep in my sleeping bag one night,
having camped in the shelter of some woods, and woke suddenly
to find that the tent had collapsed on top of me. I scrambled out
to discover that the tent lines had been broken; a herd of reindeer

trotting off were obviously guilty. I could only laugh at this experience. As a rule I find that the intimate contact with nature and wildlife is one of the rich rewards of sleeping out in the open.

I am so very grateful that I have been gifted with good health. I had felt utter exhaustion on so many occasions, and there were times when I felt I could not have cycled another mile, but after a good night's sleep I would wake up as if nothing had happened, feeling as fit as a fiddle and quite ready to set off once more. I have always regarded my physical fitness as a great gift, and something that I should always make use of. Some people have very clear vocations – like the Reverend Colin Horne, whom I hold in such great esteem, and others like him who are so naturally gifted with the ability to spread the word of Our Lord. In my case I firmly believe that I have been put on this earth to help others by raising money for charity in the only way I can. I suppose it is this belief which helps me to keep going, and why

The outdoor life.

it *never* occurs to me to give up or abandon hope. Even when I became giddy and dizzy from sheer exhaustion (and that happened on more than one occasion) I was always driven by the knowledge of other people's suffering and hardship. A short rest, a drink, or in some cases an overnight stop, and off I would go again, my will power never failing, and my determination to finish the task I had set myself spurring me ever onwards. Often the going was rough, but I cycled to the summit of every mountain I came across – never once did I get off and push the bike – and the feeling of achievement each time provided the impetus for the next challenge.

There were many high spots on this trip; glorious moments alone at the top of a mountain, breathing in the clear, pure air and gazing at the unspoilt vista beyond, or moments shared with other people, who welcomed me into their midst, ensuring that never once did I feel a stranger; but there were awkward and unpleasant moments too. I have never wanted to live a life of luxury, and can often willingly do without the creature comforts that I know many people consider to be necessities, but often the practical problems I faced were hard to deal with. One example was the problem of washing. I carried too many warm clothes with me, really, as I had not been too sure how cold I would get. Nevertheless, I still had to wash my clothes, and this I would do in the evening, in the hope that they would be dry by morning. More often than not, they were still wet, and I have to say I find the experience of getting dressed in damp clothes *extremely* unpleasant. Because space was limited, I could not carry much food with me. Bread, sardines and cheese were my staple diet, but that can become tedious after a while. However, my goal remained clear, and the motivation to keep going was undaunted throughout the entire trip. It never once occurred to me to abandon my plan, even when I was being attacked by thousands of angry mosquitoes, or when I was struggling with a pair of wet socks in the cold light of the morning.

I was very fortunate in that I only lost one item throughout the entire journey – and that was my sleeping bag. This had happened further south, when there was more traffic about: I was riding through a very busy tunnel when my sleeping bag became dislodged and fell from the back of the bicycle. The sheer volume of traffic, and the fact that I was in a tunnel at the time, made it impossible to stop, and I could only continue, helplessly, as my poor sleeping bag became swallowed up in the stream of vehicles coming up behind me. On reaching the camp site that night I explained my predicament and was able to borrow a duvet for the night. The following day I bought a brand new sleeping bag, and secured it tightly to the bike. It was later that same day that I actually saw a man dislodging the remains of my old sleeping bag from underneath his Volvo.

From Tana, I faced the last leg of my journey. I was now heading west, towards Kirkenes, which is right on the border of Russia, or what was then the Soviet Union. Here, the 'road' was often no more than just loose stone and rock, which made cycling extremely difficult and quite hazardous. Motorists were always very courteous, slowing down and giving me a wide berth. Maybe that is because they are so unused to cyclists in Norway, but British motorists could certainly learn a thing or two from them. I had been going for about 80 miles along this road (still the E6) and was beginning to feel quite tired. At the side of the road, large signs appeared, and in English I read:

WARNING

Military Restricted Area
No stopping for 11 km
No photographs

There was no way I could have cycled another 11 km without first having a rest, so I pulled the bike to the side of the road and drank thirstily from my bottle. I had recently filled this from a waterfall, and the water tasted delicious – really pure and quite sweet. I sat quietly for about 25 minutes, gathering my energy for the stretch ahead. Suddenly the silence was disturbed by the sound of wheels crunching on gravel; I looked up to see a military jeep pulling up just beside me. Two or three soldiers got out and walked slowly towards me. They were not aggressive in their manner, but were clearly asking what I was doing there. I answered as best I could, but my explanation only met with blank expressions. I resorted to universal "army language", and was eventually able to get the message across! It was only at this point that the officer in charge began speaking to me in perfect English. I don't understand why he didn't address me in English at first, or why they pretended not to understand me when I was speaking to them, but maybe I had to convince them that I was not a spy! As we got chatting, they all seemed to be very interested in what I was doing, and then one of them produced a flask from the jeep and offered me a cup of coffee. After sharing their coffee I mounted my bike and set off along the road, with their good wishes ringing in my ears.

As I approached the Russian border, the mountains gradually began to disappear. Gentle rolling hills took the place of snow-capped peaks; it was a different sort of beauty, less stark and threatening, and I really enjoyed that last stretch of the ride.

I had a letter for the Mayor of Kirkenes, too, from the Mayor of Tunbridge Wells, and I was greeted warmly by the local officials and presented with a fine plaque. Of course I had to incorporate a visit to the border itself. In my original plans for this trip I had wanted to ride over the border and cycle through part of the Soviet Union, but the bureaucracy involved became far too much of a headache. The Prime Minister's Private Secretary had herself given me a word of caution about venturing across the border, and visa applications and other forms to fill in would have taken up so much time that I decided in the end to give up. However, I had got as far as the border, and this was my ultimate destination. Barbed wire and land mines did not exactly create an impression of warmth, or make you feel welcome. I felt quite saddened by the sight; tall towers where soldiers with rifles stood on perpetual guard, and prohibitive, man-made barriers. After such a pleasant, friendly experience in Norway this all came as a bit of a shock; I couldn't help but feel that if only these barriers could be dismantled, the people could all live as one. Seeing such obvious signs of man's intervention in the world certainly makes you question all sorts of issues about politics, and war, and man's inhumanity to man. The Soviet guard who stood unsmilingly at the barrier had his camera pointed in my direction at one point. I don't suppose I shall ever see a copy of that particular 'happy snap' – it is probably in some official file gathering dust somewhere.

Kirkenes was my final destination, and I now had to consider the journey home. There are no trains in this part of the world, so my only option was to fly back down to Oslo. I cycled off to the 'airport', which I have to say resembled a small car park rather than any airfield I have ever seen. A couple of tiny planes sat on the tarmac – so small they looked like toys. The plane that was to take me back to Oslo could only carry ten passengers, and I had to dismantle the bike completely in order to get it on the plane. I removed the pedals, lowered the saddle and turned the handlebars round in the hope that it would fit into the tiny aircraft. With the help of a willing steward, and with much push-ing and shoving, we finally got it into the hold. I must say it felt rather degrading for my poor bike to be treated in this manner after it had served me so well for 2,500 miles.

I had to change planes six times before finally arriving at Gatwick Airport on 23 July – two weeks ahead of my original schedule. It was ironically on this last exhausting journey of over 18 hours that my bike had its one and only puncture. Tyres have to be deflated before a bike is allowed onto a plane, because of the problems of altitude and pressure. I had to leave the bike in the care of stewards for most of the trip, and one of them must have wheeled the bike over a nail, because when I was at last reunited with it the tyre was completely flat.

It was absolutely marvellous to arrive home, and be met by all my friends and family. The first thing I did on my arrival was to look and see how many letters I had received. Throughout the whole trip I had kept in touch with those at home via Radio Kent, and had, through my radio contact, received many good wishes and much encouragement. Now I was completely overwhelmed to find how much support I had been given. Money had come pouring in from all sorts of people, with hundreds of letters of support from Radio Kent listeners. What I found most touching were the letters from pensioners, and others who could ill afford to spare any money at all. Some people sent £1.00, apologising for the small amount but explaining that that was all they could afford. It was these letters that I found most moving; I am always so overwhelmed by people's generosity and selflessness. It is human qualities like this that, in my opinion, make such trips so thoroughly worthwhile. *Hospice at Home* received a total of £30,000 for the trip, and the organisation continues to flourish and provide a splendid service for the people of Kent. I was to spend many long hours writing my replies to all the letters I had received.

On the Tuesday after my arrival home I returned to my original starting point – Tunbridge Wells. Here I was greeted by the mayor and the now customary band of newspaper photographers and reporters. It was a moving moment indeed to hand over the plaque that had been given to me all those miles away in Kirkenes. What a different world it all seemed, now I was back here in the familiar surroundings of Tunbridge Wells, but of course, it was not long before I was back looking at maps again, and planning yet another trip. Bigger and better than ever, this time, and definitely something that no one had ever tackled before!

Chapter Seven

To Kathmandu

I DECIDED, in the end, to head for Everest. The top of the world – what could be more of a challenge, and what better way to capture the imagination of potential sponsors? Raising money for charity was of course the main aim, but I confess that I myself needed the challenge; it is in my nature, and the more I was told the idea was a ridiculous one, the more determined than ever I became to get there and prove them all wrong!

I spent months preparing for the trip. I was again going to ride for *Hospice at Home*, and my days were divided between writing letters for sponsorship (literally thousands), and reading up as much as possible on Nepal. Trekking in the Himalayas is a reasonably well-researched subject, and there is a considerable amount of literature available, offering advice on what to take, what to expect on arrival, various health precautions etc. Nowhere did I find any mention of the suitability of the tracks in the mountains for cycling, but it did not really occur to me before the trip, that not only was I the first British person ever to contemplate taking a bicycle to Everest, but probably the first person in the world. Of course, many would say it is just typical of the hairbrained ventures I think up – that Dave Wellman, he must be *mad*, wanting to take a bicycle up Everest, and at his age too! So many people asked me, before and after the trip, what on earth possesses me to do such things – they just cannot understand it. My only response to them is that *I* just cannot understand why people want to commute to work every day – to me, that seems the most boring thing in the world. Still, that is the way many people choose to lead their lives. It just so happens that I choose to have adventures. It is, for me, a way of life.

Failure was not inconceivable. I knew the trip was going to be the hardest thing I had tackled so far, and that it would be fraught with danger. I felt that I could have accepted failure, if it were the result of some vindictive twist of fate impossible to foresee, but to fail as the result of some error of judgement, or because I was too lazy or too cocksure to have researched my subject thoroughly, would be inexcusable, and so my preparations were meticulous. Before I set off I think I must have been one of England's greatest authorities on the subject of trekking in Nepal.

One of the many thousands of letters I wrote was to the Gurkha Regiment Headquarters, in London, and I received a very prompt reply from Lieutenant Colonel C N Fraser, who invited me to meet him at his office in London. I went along, one cold day in November, and found him very helpful indeed; as a result of this meeting, the arrangements for my arrival in Nepal were well taken care of. I find that the preparations for a trip such as this are exciting in themselves; it is possible to get quite caught up in this voyage of discovery, learning all sorts of things that you have never even thought of before, and meeting people from many different walks of life.

Before I left I happened to bump into the Reverend Colin Horne, the vicar of St Mary the Virgin Church in Kemsing. I have known Colin for some time, and he took the time to stop and chat about my proposed trip. As we said goodbye to one another, Colin turned to me and said, with the deepest sincerity: "Don't worry Dave. I shall be saying a prayer for you." I was to remember his words, and found them very consoling on certain occasions in the future.

At last, the many months of preparation were over, and I was ready to depart.

My starting point was again Tunbridge Wells, where the mayor formally set me on my way. I was escorted to Sevenoaks by a colourful and cheerful band of cyclists, and we made quite a sight, with flags and banners flying as we set off on our way. This group were themselves being sponsored, and collecting money along the way. It all helped in the final total, and also helped to make people feel involved. The first stop was Tonbridge, where I was again greeted by the mayor, who wished me well, and then, on my arrival in Sevenoaks, I met with a tremendous turnout in the High Street. The Mayor of Sevenoaks, Mr Maurice Short, was there, with a bevy of photographers and newspaper reporters, and crowds of people lining the streets. To my surprise, I was told that a reception had been laid on at the Council Offices; to my even greater surprise Mr Short announced that he wanted to *cycle* the distance to the Council Offices from the High Street. I willingly lent him my old racing bike (I had, for the first time, given up the racer for this trip, and was taking a mountain bike with me instead) and off he went, to the sound of much shouting and cheering. Half way down the hill, calamity struck. The chain came off (the bicycle chain that is; the mayorial chain of office still hung intact about Mr Short's neck) and the mayor came to an abrupt halt. The incident caused much mirth amongst the crowd, and Mr Short was very good natured about it. A schoolboy following behind quickly offered the use of his own bike as a replacement; Mr Short mounted and completed the rest of the journey safely, while I repaired the damage on my machine and joined him a moment later.

I was treated to a grand spread at the Council Offices; all the local dignitaries were there, as well as the press, and it made me feel really quite important! At last, all the formalities over, I was able to set off on my way to Gatwick. Someone told me they expected a car to be following with all my luggage, but I was only taking essential equipment, and *that* I was able to carry myself. Essential, for me, means of course spare inner tubes, spare tyres, spokes, and a bicycle pump in good working order. Also my tent and sleeping bag, and a spare set of clothes. Everything else I knew I would be able to acquire out there. It seemed pointless taking large amounts of food and supplies, when such provisions could be purchased there, and probably at a much cheaper price.

The flight to Kathmandu took sixteen hours, and we stopped in Frankfurt and Dubai. There were rows of empty seats on the plane: a symptom of the fact that the Gulf War was looming, and very few people were travelling. The international situation didn't give me too much cause for concern; I was delighted to have most of the plane to myself, and have room to stretch out and doze!

On stepping out of the plane I immediately recognised the meaning of the term "Culture Shock". The place was bustling with people, a heavy, rather sweet smell hung in the air, and there was a cacophony of noise. Most of the people seemed to be Indian, and as I emerged from the formalities of customs and passport control, I was greeted by a tight, heaving group of men offering:

"Taxi! Taxi!"

"Where you go?"

"I take you good hotel!"

"You come with me. I have very nice taxi!"

"Mister, here mister, I take your bags!"

Luckily I was able to shake my head to all of these offers, and made my way to a waiting Land Rover, where a Gurkha in uniform stood to attention by the open passenger door.

"Good afternoon, Sir. Welcome to Nepal," was his well-mannered, softly spoken greeting.

Once in the Land Rover, we set off with a lurch, and drove at what I thought to be far too dangerous a speed through the narrow, cluttered streets of Kathmandu. I realised, rather anxiously, that there was no seat belt in the vehicle. It occurred to me on that journey that I had not done my homework for the trip as thoroughly as I should have. Which side of the road do they drive on in Nepal? It certainly was not possible to tell from the way my driver was careering from one side to the other, swerving to avoid the occasional cow that had sat down in the middle of the road, or the pedestrians who just seemed to step out from the roadside without looking in any direction at all. Certainly no Green Cross Code in *this* place, I thought. There was an amazing amount of activity in those crowded, narrow streets; cars, buses, trucks, barrows – vehicles of all descriptions, and people everywhere, weaving in between, with children, and chickens and all manner of living things creating such a hubbub of noise – I felt completely bemused.

We arrived, at last, at the Gurkha Transit Camp, which was an oasis of calm compared to the turmoil outside. Here I was saluted and greeted with all the formality befitting a commissioned officer, and the Gurkhas seemed very honoured indeed to have me with them. That evening I was treated to an excellent curry dinner, and then shown to my room, which was quite a palatial affair with a large four-poster bed. This was draped with an overhanging mosquito net, and my first thought was that I was going to suffer a recurrence of the worst problem in Norway – the ubiquitous mosquito. Fortunately, however, I was not troubled with them at all throughout the entire trip. Perhaps it was the wrong season.

I was asked by one of the Gurkhas what time I would require my early morning tea. I asked to be woken as soon as it was light, as this is the time that I usually like to get up. I had an early night, that night, and dropped off to sleep very quickly, my head full of all the new sights and sounds and experiences I had had that day. I must have slept very heavily, for I remember nothing until I was woken, in the grey light of dawn, by a smartly dressed Ghurka standing to attention at the foot of my bed. He was holding a stainless steel beaker, and said very politely, "Your tea, Sir." I grunted an acknowledgement, and, not yet fully awake, turned over to doze for a little longer. It must have been a good half-hour before I opened my eyes again, only to see the Gurkha still standing stiffly to attention at the foot of the bed. I thought that I had dismissed him earlier, but again said "Thank you very much." Clearly this was not enough. Still the Gurkha stood there, arms stiffly by his side, chest out, eyes straight ahead. Quickly I ascertained the problem, and put the piping hot beaker of tea to my lips.

"That's fine, thank you very much," I said, having taking a sip, and with that, he wheeled an about turn and smartly left the room.

Breakfast that morning consisted of a large bowl of porridge, followed by rice and eggs. Delicious! I was informed that at 11 o'clock I would be meeting my two guides, and sure enough, at eleven on the dot two Sherpas were shown in. I had been expecting two rather slightly-built individuals, but these were quite big, strapping lads, and I felt quite relieved, knowing that they had a gruelling task ahead. I listened as the interpreter lectured them quite strongly on how they should look after me well, as I was a guest of the Gurkha Regiment. We agreed what supplies and luggage they would carry, and how much I would pay them. This amounted to about 80p a day – peanuts, for us, but a very reasonable wage for them.

The names of my two porters were Awa and Ela, and as we shook hands that morning, there began a deep friendship which I hope will endure for the rest of all our lives.

I should like to provide a bit more detail about the Sherpas; as well as the two who were to accompany me on my trail, I was to meet many others on the way, and to learn much about their remarkable way of life.

"Sherpa" means "people from the East". The Sherpas first entered Nepal from Tibet about four centuries ago. After the Chinese Occupation of Tibet in 1950, many more fled across the border, and settled further up in the Himalayan mountain range. Used to living at high altitudes, it was these settlers who found work as guides or porters (as they are often called), for the

Moving House, Sherpa Style.

Nepalese children with their pencils.

increasingly popular trekking expeditions in the Himalayas. The Sherpas are used to carrying immense loads up and down the valleys of the Himalaya, and it is not unusual to see Sherpas carrying such bulky items as furniture or building materials on their backs. No lorries can climb up to their villages; they have adapted in the best way possible to their situation, and even the youngest boys will offer their services as porters for the trekkers. For under £1.00 a day, a Sherpa will happily carry a load of over 70 kilos on his back, often in a large, wicker basket known as a "doko".

The Sherpas are a deeply spiritual people. Compared to the civilised western world, they have very little in the way of material goods. I had with me some pencils that I gave as presents to some of the Sherpa children I met – and they were as delighted with these as a British child might be if presented with a computer! But although their lives are materially simple, they are, in many other ways, rich – far richer than many I can think of at home in Britain – and they are a profoundly happy race. I was to learn over the next month how much they respect their environment; they know only too well how dangerous it can be on the mountain, and their lifestyle is dominated by their external conditions. This respect permeates every aspect of their lives, and very little happens without the advice or guidance of the Tibetan Lama, or Priest, as I was soon to find out first hand.

First, however, I had other business to conduct in Kathmandu. That evening, I had been invited to dinner with Colonel Mike Allen, at the British Embassy. As well as being the Commander of the British Gurkhas in Nepal, Colonel Allen was also the Defence Attaché, and I guess he must spend a great deal of his time conversing about military and official matters. He and his wife were most charming and he told me he was delighted to be able to talk about something non-military, for a change. We chatted very easily; I was plied with gin and tonics and then waited on at table by their houseboy. We had a very tasty meal, but the meat was unfamiliar. Lean and tender, and quite sweet to taste, it reminded me very strongly of the reindeer meat that I had sampled in Lapland. My host informed me that it was yak, at which I expressed surprise – I had read, in several sources, that one is never supposed to touch yak meat in Nepal. Colonel Allen laughed, and said that *his* had been quite hygienically prepared, but that my sources were correct: once I was on the trail, I should *never* touch the meat, no matter how tempting it looked.

We continued chatting easily, after dinner was over; I was offered more gin and tonics and the conversation flowed. At 11 o'clock I was told that my driver was ready. I said farewell to the Colonel, who wished me luck and said he would see me on my return, and then I was whisked back through the narrow streets of the city to the Ghurka Rest House.

I spent the following day wandering around the colourful, noisy streets of Kathmandu, gathering together the final items I needed for my trip, changing travellers cheques, and making a few last minute preparations. I telephoned my wife, Olive, to let her know that I had arrived safely, and told her to pass on all the information of my whereabouts to the press and radio, who might be calling her for news. I knew this would be the last time we would speak for some while; there is nowhere in Nepal, outside Kathmandu, to make an international telephone call. Even here, in the city, it was quite a business; there are no telephone kiosks as such, but instead a single shop, which contains a row of booths. You have to go to the counter and tell them the number you need to call, and then you are allotted a certain booth from which to make your call.

Walking through the streets of Kathmandu is certainly an interesting experience. The contents of all the little shops spill out onto the roadside, and a mixture of sweet and spicy smells fills the air. There are people everywhere, and the traffic weaves its way in and out of the various obstacles, horns blaring, people shouting, dogs barking. Pagodas and temples, domes and shrines and slender pillars of gods and kings adorned with finely intricate wood carvings or gold filigree, appear between the ramshackle huts that serve as shops and houses.

I spent three nights in all with the Gurkhas, which enabled me to get acclimatised. They were really very helpful, and provided me with a great deal of useful information about what I should take, what I should do, and the customs I should observe on my journey. The Nepalese are a very polite people, and even if you learn no more of the language, the one word that *every* traveller will remember is "Namaste". This is the universal greeting, "Hello", "How are you?" "How do you do?" "Pleased to meet you," "Good morning", etc., etc. It is always accompanied by the gesture of placing the palms together in front of you, fingers pointing in the air, and we used this greeting to everyone that we met along the trail.

Setting out on the trail, I overtake some yaks.

Nepalese children have their first sighting of a bicycle.

Chapter Eight

Into the Himalayas

WHEN THE DAY DAWNED for our departure, the Sherpas
loaded up their packs and set off at a reasonable walking pace. I must add that my need to prepare and
acclimatise had not been the only factors taken into consideration when planning our departure date. In Nepal, there are only
certain days of the week on which it is considered auspicious to
embark on a journey, and Sherpas will never set out on a Sunday.
This is a bad day, and any journey beginning on a Sunday will
end with blood. The same applies to Tuesday, while anything
undertaken on a Wednesday will take a long time to finish. Friday
is considered to be a good day, especially for travellers, and likewise
a Monday. So, on a clear Monday morning, Awa, Ela and myself
set out to travel from Kathmandu to Everest Base Camp.

I cycled out of Kathmandu, and as far along the track as I
could, with my Sherpas at times in front, at times behind. The
track soon gave way to impassable terrain, however, with rocks
and boulders littering the path, and the path itself becoming at
times impossibly narrow. I was forced to dismount and carry the
bike across my shoulders. I think that, in all, I cycled only for
about 20% of the entire trip, but having the bike with me was
an interesting starting point for many conversations; many of the
people we were to meet along our route lived in such remote
areas that they had never seen a bicycle before in their lives. I
was always surrounded by a cluster of intrigued people, usually
children, wanting to touch the machine and discover how it
worked. I also attracted attention on account of my grey hair,

which is very rarely seen out there. The Sherpa people have a
relatively short life span, the average life expectancy being 52
years. I believe this is because of the altitude, which also affects
their growth – as a race they are considerably smaller than people
from the West.

I had planned my first overnight stop to be at a place called
Tiri, which is situated at 6,726 feet above sea level. However, I
did not make nearly such good time as I thought I would, mainly
because I stopped to talk to so many of the locals on the way. It
was great, though, and I was not at all bothered. The people are
all so friendly and welcoming, and their gentle smiles are really
heartwarming. We got as far as Lamosangu, that night, and
pitched our tents for our first night under canvas.

The next morning, one of my Sherpas told me that he had to
go and see the Tibetan priest.

"Fine by me," I said. "Whatever makes you happy!"

I wondered whether they doubted the wisdom of my trip, and
was concerned that they did not think we would make it to
Everest. Anyway, off he went, and returned sometime later grinning from ear to ear.

"Tomorrow you see priest," he said to me. "Lama like to see
you. You must go, or Makula God angry."

I agreed, not wanting to upset the chap, and the following
morning was taken to a monastery situated on the hillside. The
place reeked of incense. I was greeted by the priest, who carefully
placed a hand on each of my shoulders, then touched my head,
shook a few beads, and muttered some words under his breath.
Then he said to my Sherpas, in English:

"He is very brave and good man. No harm will come to him,
and he will protect you. Makula God is a real God. A big God,
and he is happy with you."

Both Awa and Ela looked immensely relieved on hearing these
words, everyone was smiling as we said Cheerio, and off we went
once again.

I feel that it is always of the utmost importance – not to mention courteous – to respect the traditions, customs and beliefs of the people I am with. The Sherpas' way of life, and the emphasis they place on ceremony and belief, was something that was to colour my experience throughout. I have mentioned briefly the background of the Sherpa culture; perhaps here I could add a little bit more about their way of life, based on experiences I had whilst on the trail:

We had only been travelling for a few days, and, with evening approaching, the time was right to find somewhere to camp for the night. I saw a spendid spot ahead; it looked fairly sheltered, and the ground did not look too rocky or hard.

"How about there?" I suggested to my two guides.

Ala looked extremely anxious, and said very quickly,

"Over there no good. Better we go on."

There was an urgency in his voice that I found quite puzzling. I asked him why we could not stop in the place I had suggested.

"Many spirits there," came the response. "No good for our journey".

I had no choice but to accept that he knew better than I did on this one.

I was also to learn about the rituals surrounding birth, marriage and death – events that are associated with ceremony in any culture, but in Nepal the traditions are vastly different from our own.

Eleven days after a baby is born, a priest will call at the house to name the baby. The name given by priest is determined by the day, the month and the year of the baby's birth; a marker of twigs or some such is then placed on the roof of the house to indicate that the naming ceremony has taken place. After the baby has been named by the priest, it is given a second name by its parents. This second name is the name that is used; the name given by the priest remains a closely guarded secret. Knowing that all Sherpas have two names, I asked several people what their 'other' name

A married Sherpa woman showing off her apron.

was. But every time, I was given only a broad smile and a shake of the head. No one must ever be told the secret name.

When a Sherpa woman gets married, she does not have a ring, as in our culture. She is given, instead, an apron, usually brightly coloured, which she must then wear. A married woman is thus recognised by her apron: I am sure there are a few women in England who might have a thing or two to say about *that*! I bought one of these aprons as a souvenir to bring home with me – it was the only memento I purchased throughout the whole trip, as I was limited by space. Although the taking of more than one wife is permitted, it is extremely rare. If a married Sherpa should die, the younger brother has the right to marry his older brother's widow, and the younger sister has the right to marry her deceased elder sister's husband.

I recall very vividly at one point along the route, some way up a mountain, we stopped for a short rest. Looking down into the valley below, I could see that a large crowd had assembled, many of whom seemed to be Lama (priests). When I asked what was going on, my Sherpas informed me that a funeral was taking place. I was very curious. They could not possibly be going to bury the body, as the ground consisted of hard rock. I assumed that they would cremate it. I asked my two friends, who clearly did not understand the meaning of the word "cremation".

"Will they burn the body?" I asked, trying to make my meaning clear.

The Sherpas looked horrified.

"Oh no," they exclaimed, and then they proceeded to tell me what happens.

The body is first of all cut up. The Lama then consults his book, and according to the time of death, the pieces will either be thrown into the river, or scattered on the mountain. This disperses the spirit. The pieces are then consumed by the "giddha", or bearded vulture. I caught sight of this bird one day; with a wing span of 8–10 feet it is an impressive sight – it glides around the mountain tops, circling on the air currents, and silhouetted against the sky.

Another impressive Himalayan bird is the Black Eagle. I remember seeing one circling above me the first time that the white mountains of the Himalayas came into view. I was absolutely spellbound; the giant peaks rose majestically way, way into the distance, peak after peak after peak, stretching silent and awesome as far as the eye could see with the black bird silently silhouetted against the brilliant blue sky.

The scenery changes very rapidly in the foothills. Lower down, there is intense cultivation: green rice, golden buckwheat, potatoes and sweetcorn are grown in profusion, and the terraced hillsides are a picturesque riot of verdant colour. The rhododendron is native to the Himalayan foothills and provides a deep

Greeted by Nepalese policemen with flowers.

splash of colour amongst the different greens. I understand that
the flower is eaten as a cure for tummy upsets. I recall one day
being approached by five Nepalese policemen, all carrying guns
which were slung over their shoulders. I felt quite apprehensive
as they came closer, but then noticed that they were all carrying
bunches of rhododendron flowers in their hands. News of my
arrival had reached them and they came to congratulate me and
wish me well. We happened to be nearby a tea house at the time,
and sat down together for a drink and a chat. Unfortunately I
had to the leave the large and very beautiful bunches of flowers
behind; I could not manage them *and* the bike.

The paths in the lower foothills were well-worn and easy to
follow. The only bits I found tricky were some of the rope
bridges which crossed the rivers. These were often rotten, and in
a bad state of repair. The wooden slats were frequently riddled

A variety of bridges to cross in the Himalayan foothills.

with woodworm, and the solution in many cases was just to place another piece of wood over the original, rotten one.

There are many different tracks throughout the foothills of the Himalayas, and one often comes across group of people heading in one direction or another, all with their Sherpa guides. I often found that the people we encountered knew that we were on our way long before our arrival. The local 'bush telegraph' is a highly effective means of communication; travellers up and down the mountain always stop to chat and in this way news is passed quickly in both directions.

In the lower foothills, the fields and terraces are interspersed with small settlements. The clay houses often have thatched roofs, although sometimes sheets of corrugated iron serve as a covering instead, and the houses nestle together in small clusters. Women in brightly coloured costume gather to draw water from the well – taps have recently been introduced, and they no longer have to drop a bucket to collect their water. Woodsmoke rises, but not from chimneys; inside the houses the smoke fills the room and finds its way out through whatever crack, crevice or opening it can. All along the route we came across isolated shacks and many tea houses, where it is possible to partake of a drink of yak milk. Everything inside these houses is black, on account of the smoke. Although wood is burnt lower down the valley, the staple fuel higher up the mountain is dried yak dung. The pats burn slowly, and give out a very strong, perfumed smell, which is not in itself unpleasant, although it is rather offputting knowing its origins. The smell would linger on your clothes for days afterwards.

As we were walking slowly up the path one day, me with my bicycle slung across my shoulders, the Sherpas with their heavy loads bent forward under the weight, Ela asked me if we could call in on a friend of his. I agreed readily, but there was not a house in sight and I wondered what he could mean. We continued walking for another couple of hours, and then a small hut came into view, some way off the path. Ela pointed excitedly, and said that that was where his friend lived. Surrounding the hut was a large group of yak, who shuffled rather crossly as we attempted to get through. Yak dung littered the ground all around the hut; it was messy and very smelly. The hut was very small, stone built, and with a sheet of corrugated iron for a roof. Laid out on the ground around the hut were large bamboo mats covered with salt, placed there to dry. As we entered the dark interior, the stench of dung was overwhelming. A large pot hung over a wood fire – it contained yak milk, and once it came to the boil, a dirty cup was used to ladle out the milk into tin mugs. We were invited to sit down, and my Sherpa moved an old blanket to give me more room; as he did so a swarm of black flies flew buzzing into the air. Yet despite the seemingly dirty conditions, it was warm and dry, and the hospitality was wonderful. Ela's friend seemed delighted to see all of us, and we sat and talked for hours, consuming several mugs of hot, sweet yak milk. No sugar is added, incidentally, the yak milk being naturally sweet.

We often stopped for a cup of yak milk at one of the tea houses along the route. We also used it to make our porridge, which we had for breakfast every day. Apart from that my diet consisted of "daal bhaat", or rice with a few vegetables. Rice for dinner, rice for tea, every day; but I was hungry, and it was always welcome, (especially as, higher up the mountain, the food could take a good two hours to heat up properly) and I also knew, more importantly, that it was safe. You have to be so careful with what you eat out there, and I did not want my journey ruined by a dose of "Delhi Belly" or "Kathmandu Quickstep" which curtails the trip of many a trekker.

I often recalled the words of Colonel Allen, and his advice about yak meat, for frequently I saw Sherpas along the trail, carrying yak meat in the large baskets on their backs. When they stopped to rest, they would always lay the pieces of meat out on a rock, leaving one Sherpa to squat beside the rock and casually swat any passing flies with a small stick, that seemed to be totally inadquate for the task.

There is quite an interesting story surrounding yak meat, and the Sherpas' attitude to it. The slaughter of animals for meat is again very ritualistic. The Sherpas will only kill animals with the safeguard of a Buddhist prayer, and then only on certain days. Tibetans will tour round the settlements and villages, for the ritualistic killing of animals. The carcasses are then hung inside the houses all year round, during which time, of course, they dry and shrivel.

When I had eventually reached Base Camp, and pitched my tent, I heard a terrific commotion outside. In the next group of tents some Japanese trekkers were preparing for the ascent of Everest; my Sherpas informed me that our neighbours had been preparing and cooking meat.

"This is why we have much snow and storm," they explained.

The cooking of meat at Base Camp is strictly taboo.

We went outside to see what was happening. A Tibetan priest was asking everyone if they had any rice balls – these are an essential ingredient in any offering to appease the gods. The Lama had set up a small altar, upon which a candle was burning. Ela and Awa joined the Sherpas of the Japanese group, who had now gathered together in front of the altar. I stood at the sidelines, a very interested spectator. The Sherpas all stood with their left palm facing inwards, little finger and forefinger pointing towards the altar. They threw rice at the candle, and began chanting a prayer. More rice was thrown, and another prayer chanted. This went on for ages – it could well have been over an hour – until the candle finally burnt itself out. I was told, afterwards, that this ceremony ensured the reincarnation of the yak soul to a higher life. As the ceremony was completed, all the Sherpas once again looked relieved and happy.

As well as meat, drinking water is another health risk in Nepal. Among the most beautiful sights in the mountains are the waterfalls which come tumbling down from great heights; sheets of sparkling, clear water glistening in the sunlight. It looks so re-freshing, and so tempting, but it would be lethal to drink. All water has to be boiled, and then sterilised with an iodine tablet. It is not worth the risk of even cleaning your teeth in unsterilised, or unboiled water.

Walking along the track that winds its way steadily up the mountain is a surprisingly sociable activity. There are always groups of trekkers that one meets along the way; some more daring and adventurous than others, but nevertheless all with a fixed goal in mind, and all enjoying the pleasure that strenuous physical exertion can bring. Everyone that I met seemed to be united by an instant bond of friendship, through the knowledge of shared experience and understanding. I therefore felt very saddened by a first-hand encounter with tragedy amongst one of the groups that I met. We had stopped to chat, as usual, my two Sherpas exchanging words with theirs and me providing all the usual stuff about the trip and the bike. They were a friendly group, but there was one young lad amongst them – late twenties, I think he was – who was complaining of a headache. I had spent so long preparing for this trip and had read and re-read the extensive chapters on 'Health' several times. I knew immediately what the cause of his headache must be.

"You must go down the mountain at once, and slowly," I urged him. "This is one of the first signs of altitude sickness."

The young man dismissed my warning lightly.

"Oh, I'll be all right," he said, breezily.

I could not be so sure. Feeling quite concerned, I went to speak to the group leader, and share my suspicions. He, too, was dis-missive, and rather offhand.

"Oh he'll be fine," he assured me. "It's only a headache."

Feeling that there was nothing more I could say, we exchanged farewells and continued on our paths, both headed up the moun-tain valley, but along different trails. Some three or four days later, I met the group again, and realised at once that their numbers were depleted. I asked how they were getting on, and they said that, although they were all fine, some of the party had decided to head back down the mountain. It turned out that the chap with the headache had crawled into his sleeping bag a few days after I saw him, and just did not wake up the following morning. Altitude sickness is *extremely* dangerous, and creeps up on you with perhaps only a headache for warning. You then begin to feel slightly dizzy, and to behave as if you were drunk, and then death comes quickly and silently during sleep. A grim business, and one which is so easily preventable; at the first sign, the *only* remedy is to descend the mountain. So many people get altitude sickness because they feel very fit, and scramble up the mountain far too quickly. It is important to take it slowly, with plenty of rests, and allow your body to adjust.

I said earlier that my two Sherpas believed that the cooking of meat at Base Camp had been the reason behind the "snow and storm". Snow was certainly not expected at that time of year, and although I had read of what to do if snowbound in the Himalayas I had not anticipated using this knowledge. Thunder and lightning up ahead led us to expect a downpour; it came as a shock when this fell as snow. And it was nothing like the light flakes that send the whole of the south east of England into a state of emergency. This was a real blizzard, driving thick white snow that covered the ground, until we were wading through drifts of up to 14 inches, and sinking knee deep in the stuff. It was impossible to keep going, and, luckily, we soon found a large rock with an overhang under which we were able to shelter. It was dry, and out of the wind, but as the light began to fade I could not help feeling anxious. Before long, it was completely dark, very cold, and eerily silent. I could feel the warmth of my two friends who sat huddled beside me, their packs resting either side of us to protect us from the wind; my bicycle leaning forlornly by the rock. I think this was the only time I really felt anything akin to fear; faced with the power of the elements in that vast and lonely space I suddenly felt very small, and vulnerable, and weak. It was then that I recalled, very strongly, the words of the Reverend Colin Horne who had spoken to me so very kindly before I left. It was as if I could actually hear his voice, and suddenly I was filled with a very deep sense of calm, and peace, and knew instinctively that all would be well. A curious experience, and one that was easy to dismiss, especially when day dawned and we were still crouching under the rock, stiff, tired, uncomfortable and very cold. Looking out from our hideaway we were confronted with complete white-out. No distinguishable features at all, just a vast white space, silent and disorientating. We had no choice but to sit it out, until, at about 10 o'clock that morning, a herd of yak came ambling through the snow, creating a track behind them as they went. Following the advice of the guide books, Ela, Awa and I gathered our belongings and quickly pursued the yak, following the path they had created for us. This was, I think, the toughest part of the trip; sinking in snow at every step, cold and uncomfortable, and with visibility very poor. My bike was cumbersome, and this was the one point where I began to wish I had left it at home. I had not been fully prepared for this extreme cold, and failed to protect my face properly. Later the skin peeled off completely. That day was really hard going. That night, as we struggled to erect our tents, the cold seemed to nail my feet through my socks. When it came to cooking, I wrestled clumsily with the stove, and my eyes misted over. I soon forgot the stove, and rummaged through my bag for the Army 24-hour ration packets, which had been supplied by the Gurkhas. I found two bars of chocolate, and ate these quickly, in an attempt to restore some energy. It was such a relief to climb into my sleeping bag that night.

On many occasions I felt the limits of my endurance were completely stretched. The narrow trail seemed endless, up and up and up, and it became a real effort to put one foot in front of the other. Every part of me ached, my eyes would not focus properly, and I felt that my body just would not take any more. It is amazing how concentrated the mind becomes when the body is pushed in this way. You fix with all your being on the next step, then the next, then the next, willing yourself to continue. I have always believed that to give up is harder than to go on, but there were some moments on that trail that, if anyone had offered, I would have accepted the chance to be carried back down the valley, and to suffer no longer. And then, somehow, it seems that you reach a kind of 'pain barrier', through which you pass and emerge feeling fresher, and brighter and fitter. Your mind is cleared, you can enjoy the views around you once more, and press on, ever upwards, feeling lighter and easier than before. To share this experience with others unites friends in a way that no other experience can. I felt a deep and lasting bond of friendship developing between myself and my two Sherpas, who were ever cheerful and willing, and never once complained.

That night underneath that rock was probably the most uncomfortable experience I had. Nights were often spent in wayside shacks or tea houses, or under canvas, or in a cave. It was often cold, but I had a good sleeping bag, and it was wonderful to be able to look up at night into the clear sky, and see the stars. It was always a great relief to take my boots off last thing at night, and relax my weary feet in the soft down of my sleeping bag. One morning, after we had spent the night in a shack, I had left my boots on the floor underneath my bed. I awoke in the morning and went to put my boots on, only to discover that they were frozen stiff. It was impossible to manipulate the leather at all, and I called on one of my trusty Sherpas to help. He grinned, and took the boots outside. Within minutes he was back, the boots clearly de-frosted, and beautifully supple. I did not ask what he had done, but the curious smell emanating from the boots was enough to give me a hint. Those Sherpas were certainly resourceful. I have to say that in future I kept my boots in my sleeping bag with me, preferring the marginal level of discomfort to having to thaw out my footwear every morning.

The Sherpas do not as a rule stay up in the mountains in the winter. They will gather their few possessions and move down the mountain, sometimes for four or five months, until the very severe weather is over. However, the old people and those who are disabled, and cannot make the trip down, remain in their villages. Although this may sound cruel, they are left with plenty of provisions and a good supply of yak dung for fuel, and are quite comfortable. If the whole family were to stay with them, there would never be enough to go round. Everyone returns for the festival of New Year (Losar) which is in February.

The Sherpas' economic system seems to thrive on two main components: expeditions like mine, and the ubiquitous yak. Like the reindeer in Lapland, the yak in the Himalaya is utilised in many ways. I was impressed by the neat piles of dried yak dung stacked up against the shacks for use in the winter, in the same way that we stack logs. Their milk is used for all dairy products, especially butter – the butter is an ingredient of the traditional salted Tibetan tea which is drunk by the Sherpas in great quantities. Yak wool is used for clothing, of course, and the women weave brightly coloured mats and rugs from yak wool which are taken down the mountain to the lower valleys. A bartering system of exchange is often used, and mats will be traded for grain and food. The Tibetans cross breed their yaks with cows and the resultant offspring are known as "Dzpkyo" (male) and "Dzum" (female). The male is ideal for carrying loads, and coping with different extremes in temperature.

The wild, pure yaks fare better in higher altitudes. They are quite magnificent beasts, heavy and stately and lumbering and gentle. They did not, however, seem to take too kindly to the bicycle, often nudging it with their horns as we passed by. One day I came across a herd of fine-looking beasts. I was carrying the bike across my shoulders, so put it down carefully in order

The photo came out well, though!

not to distract them. Often they can look quite shabby and dirty, their long hair matted and grey from the mud, but this particular group all appeared to have fine, soft, black hair, and impressive horns. I thought that the folks back home would appreciate a photograph of the leader – the largest of the group, with the most magnificent pair of horns I have ever seen. He really was a beautiful beast, and clearly a thoroughbred. I took my camera out of my bag. It is one of those idiot-proof machines that tells you that it is OK to take a picture, and I pressed the button accordingly. Beep-beep came the responding message, assuring me that I could take a photograph, no problem. Clearly the yak was not acquainted with automatic cameras and their characteristic call. At the noise he charged straight for me, pushing me to one side. I fell heavily on to the rocks, and as I picked myself up, realised that I had damaged my right arm. Not too seriously,

but enough to merit the use of a bandage for four days. I returned
bearing the scar, and related the tale to many a listener. The photo
came out well, though!

As we approached our final destination of Everest Base Camp,
travelling now across the dry, rocky ground of glacier moraine,
I was rather disturbed to see a long row of memorial stones.
These are found all along the trail, at various intervals, and it is
important to observe the local custom of only walking on the left
hand side of the stones. Usually there would be one or two stones
together, but here, the line of stones stretched nearly as far as the
eye could see – memorials to the climbers who had succumbed
to the elements, or fallen to their deaths when ascending the
peaks above. A chilling reminder of how dangerous the place
could be, and also a tribute to the intrepid spirit of human nature,
determined as ever to face a challenge, and to do something
"because it is there".

With Sir Edmund Hillary in Nepal.

One of the most memorable encounters during my trek was a chance meeting with the climber Sir Edmund Hillary – perhaps the name most often associated with Mount Everest. He often makes trips out to his beloved Nepal, and provides advice and guidance for climbing expeditions. He had heard of my trip, and we spent some time in conversation together. A disarming and unassuming chap, you could not help but get caught up in his infectious enthusiasm for the place, and I was beginning to understand why, for this great man, the Himalyas has become a consuming passion.

Before reaching my destination of Everest Base Camp, I was persuaded to deviate from the trail slightly to attempt to climb Kala Pattar. This mountain is 18,450 feet above sea level, and is about six miles directly due west of Mount Everest. I was assured that the spectacular views would be well worth the tough climb to the top. We set off that day from the settlement of Lobuche, a terrace of small stone houses nestling into the hills in between the Lobuche and vast Khumbu glaciers. I had my bicycle with me, of course, impressing my two Sherpas immensely. As we climbed sharply upwards, the change in altitude was very notice-able. It is possible to fill the lungs only half full with oxygen at such a height, and I was, near the top, only able to walk about forty yards before I had to stop and rest. We climbed up through the clouds, which was quite amazing – especially emerging the other side to clear, brilliant blue sky, the white mountain top glistening in the sunlight, and below us the cotton-wool tops of thick white cloud.

The view from the top of Kala Pattar has been described as one of the most majestic in the world. I had a clear sighting of the immense south and west faces of Everest, and just gazed for what seemed like hours across at the peaks of the Himalayan mountains, ridge after ridge, peak after peak, in an endless pattern of white against the blue sky. The sense of immense, vast, endless space was one of the most enriching experiences of the whole trip. The air stung my face with its sharpness and freshness, and I felt a very deep and lasting sense of contentment.

Kala Pattar – On top of the world with a bicycle.

Chapter Nine

Return

I RETURNED TO KATHMANDU having travelled a distance of some 250 miles. It was nothing, compared to the immense distance I had covered on my trip to Norway, or even the cycling I had done at home in Britain. But I had achieved something that no-one in the world had ever done before, and I had also discovered the limits of my own endurance, and my capacity for physical pain and suffering. It was a great personal achievement, but of course, I had not undertaken the trip for purely selfish reasons, and it really added to my feeling of exhilaration to know that I had succeeded once again in contributing in some way to those who really needed the money at home.

Back in Kathmandu, which now seemed to me to be the centre of the civilised world, I was welcomed enthusiastically by my hosts at the Gurkha Transit Camp, with broad smiles and many handshakes of congratulation. They treated me like a real hero, and I was entertained royally once again with a formal, regimental dinner and all the pomp and ceremony befitting an officer. The first night I was back, I slept soundly in a comfortable bed for the first time in over three weeks. It was blissful to have my first, refreshing shower and relax my aching muscles. The following day, feeling completely refreshed, I went off to find the little shop in Kathmandu from where I could make an international call. The streets of the hot, bustling city now felt quite comfortable and familiar, although it was a shock to see so many people after the isolation of the mountains. From my booth, I telephoned Olive, first of all, and she was delighted to hear my voice, not having had any contact at all since I had set off on the trip. I think she may have worried about me a bit on this one, although she would not admit to it! Later, back at the Transit Camp, I received a telephone call from Radio Kent. It was gone three o'clock in afternoon, but I found myself speaking on Pat Marsh's Breakfast Show, and, very briefly, began telling all those listeners about my adventures as they sat eating their cornflakes. It felt very strange having this contact with people again. I had not seen a paper, or listened to the news, or spoken to anyone about anything other than trekking for over three weeks. I cannot say that I felt in any way deprived. Nothing had mattered other than the basic priorities – where to get shelter, and food, and how to keep alive. These are the concerns of the gentle, friendly Sherpa people, and while international wars rage, and politicians argue, and the interest rate increases, and the pound floats, or sinks, or whatever, their lives continue in an unhurried, peaceful fashion. They are uncorrupted by the modern world, and they have a great gift to share, and much that we could learn from.

The time had come to say goodbye to my two faithful, hard-working and loyal Sherpas. I had shared with them some of the most gruelling experiences in my life, and I found it hard to believe that we would never meet again. I had wanted to give them my bicycle to share between them, as a thank you for their devoted service throughout the trip, and as a reminder of our friendship, but I was advised, quite seriously, by the Gurkhas, that this would not be a good idea. These people are used to the simple life, with simple pleasures. They do not recognise emotions such as jealousy, or pride, for they have nothing to be jealous or proud about. They do not hanker after material goods, for they have nothing. If I were to give them such a great gift, I would introduce all sorts of complexities and imbalances in their lives, and ultimately they would suffer. It is hard for a Westerner to understand and appreciate such concepts, but I respected what I was told, and knew, from their broad smiles, that when I said a very heartfelt and sincere "thank you" to them both, that the words were enough in themselves. I have a strong feeling that, in one way or another, Awa and Ela will always be two of my closest friends, and will remain with me for the rest of my life.

It was finally time for my departure. As the plane took off from the tarmac of Kathmandu airport, I felt mingled feelings of sadness and excitement. Sadness at leaving behind some of the most beautiful places in the world, and of saying farewell to people whom I respected and cared for, but excitement at the prospect of returning home, to friends and family, and the comforting familiarity of my house and garden. I was eager to share my experiences with the people at home, and impart to those I knew a little of the rich experience I had had on this truly remarkable adventure.

It took me some while to adjust to life back at home. It is hard to imagine just how different *everything* is, and although I had only been away for four weeks, I felt as if I was noticing everything for the first time. The quality of the light, and the different smells and feel of the air are perhaps the things you notice most sharply when first stepping out of the anonymous atmosphere of an airport terminal. Then I was suddenly aware of the size of people, and the greyness of their appearance; I had grown so used to the broad, welcoming smiles of the Nepalese and the Sherpas, and their relaxed manner, that it was quite a shock to realise how people at home hurry around without looking up, or meeting your gaze. Everyone seemed to be in such a rush, and to be so preoccupied.

Of course I was welcomed very warmly on my arrival back in my home town. I wanted to tell everyone immediately what it had been like, but it is very difficult to find the words to take in such a rich and varied experience.

You run the risk of boring people silly at first, but I was

eventually able to get all my information and stories into some sort of presentable order, and convey something of my adventures with the help of photographs and pictures.

My first task was of course to tackle all the mail that had arrived in my absence, and respond individually to all the letters I had received. I set to work immediately chasing up all the promises of money, and publicising the trip on the radio and elsewhere. I was invited to give talks to WI meetings, Baptist Churches, Friendship Clubs and British Legions. It was good for me to be able to re-live some of those experiences once more, and to share them with other people. I soon began to get into the swing of things again, and settle down to some sort of routine. But as the nights began to draw in, and the cold rains of October and November lashed against the window panes, I could not help thinking wistfully of the heat and noise and dust of Kathmandu, or the wide, vast open spaces of those glorious mountains. There was a feeling within which by now had become quite recognisable. As I was relating all my tales to eager audiences, I could feel already the yearning for adventure and discovery. Already, I needed another challenge. I began to visit my local library again, and my eyes would wander across the titles in the "Travel" section. Where could I go next?

It turned out that my next charity ride was in fact to Canterbury. Not, perhaps, the most exotic sounding of destinations, and not exactly far-flung. But the trip came about because of a very particular need. There were three people in my village of Kemsing who were suffering in very different ways. Burt Skinner was having kidney dialysis treatment. The only way he was going to be able to lead anything like a normal life again was to have a machine installed at his home – otherwise he ran the risk of being almost permanently in hospital. Such machines cost a vast sum of money, and there was no way that Burt could afford this. Then there was Chris Lane, who badly needed the computer that would enable her to write. *That* cost something like £3,200. Then

Philip Baldwin, severely handicapped, who had found out about a specially designed armchair that he would be able to sit in. As a village, we got together, and thought hard about how we could help these people. I suggested a fun cycle ride, and the idea was eagerly taken up.

So on a freezing cold day in December myself and four others set off, with Colin Horne there to see us off and wish us well. It was 9.15 in the morning; ice still covered the roads and we could see our breath in front of us as we pedalled along, but our spirits were high; we were not striving to beat any records, but merely enjoy the outing. Later on in the morning the sun broke through, and it really was a pleasant ride. I must say it felt quite a relief to be bowling along the firm tarmac of reliable British roadways. I thought back, briefly, to the rocky terrain of the winding mountain tracks in the Himalayas. What a lifetime ago that seemed to me now.

We sailed through the castle walls of Canterbury at 1.45 p.m. that day, breathless from our ride, and eager for a refreshing lunch in one of the many pubs in the city.

A total of £2,600 was raised; not only did the ride help three very needy individuals, but it also served another, very important purpose, in bringing together the hearts and minds of the local community. The Sherpa communities of the Himalayas are bound by many shared values, and a commitment and an understanding that is often not found in English communities. Individuals are often isolated, in this country, and have no shared sense of purpose. If, in undertaking our trip to Canterbury, we had brought a little of the Sherpa mentality to Kemsing, then I think it might have become, in some way, a better place to be.

Chapter Ten

Death Valley

TIMBUCTOO IS ONE OF THOSE PLACES that, since my child-
hood, has conjured up notions of the mysterious, the
exciting and the exotic. It has to do with exploration, and
adventure and challenge. It sounded just the place for me. I went
to my atlas – I couldn't even be sure where Timbuctoo *was*. I
planned my route, and began all the usual business of letter-writ-
ing, and approaching the various embassies. It was here, unfortunately, that I came unstuck. There was a lot of muttering and
shaking of heads, and I received several rather unenthusiastic
letters advising me of all the problems inherent in my proposed
trip. What finally dissuaded me was the letter that came announc-
ing that I would *have* to take an escort with me. I am not
insensitive to diplomatic language and, reading between the lines,
realised that this meant, in effect, that I was being advised not to
undertake the venture. I took the advice on board, and went back
to my atlas. Where else had such an adventurous sounding name
as Timbuctoo? The map fell open on the United States of America, and I glanced across, at California, and the neighbouring state
of Nevada, home of the notorious Death Valley. The name alone
was enough to get me going. I took out books from the library,
wrote to the American Embassy, and soon the preparations were
well underway again.

Death Valley is, of course, well-known for its hostile conditions. In the summer, temperatures there can average a scorching
116°. I was planning to leave in November, when it should only
be around 91°. Maps of the area show a clearly marked route

running from north to south of the valley. There are many stops for tourists along the way, the largest being the Furnace Creek Visitor Center – but these cater for visitors in cars. The bicycle would be a rare sight indeed. Of course, always needing just that extra little challenge, I wasn't confining myself to the north/south route alone. I intended to cycle from the east to the west of Death Valley, too. Someone asked me, before I left, why on earth I wanted to do that.

"The reason," I told them simply, "is that no one has ever done it before."

By the middle of November the many days of preparation were over, and I was ready to set off, full of the excitement of a new adventure, and looking forward to new experiences. Before leaving Sevenoaks I met the mayor, who was now Merilyn Canet, and who gave me a goodwill message for the Mayor of Las Vegas. My first port of call was Bromley, and here too, the mayor, Dorothy Laird JP, passed on a message of goodwill to the Mayor of Las Vegas.

Members of the MS Group see me on my way.

My goal was to raise £18,000 for a much-needed ambulance for the MS group and it was a fine moment when the group turned out to see me off on my 1,200-mile ride.

I flew from Gatwick Airport with North West Airlines, and we had a very good flight. I was to catch a connecting flight in Minneapolis to Las Vegas, but here I found that the next fight had been cancelled and I was obliged to wait for five and a half hours. This gave me plenty of time to look around; the transit lounge was a swish area of glass plate and neon, and full of people rushing here, there and everywhere. My first impressions of the American people was their size; they are noticeably bigger, on average, than the British. Many of the young girls, especially, seemed overweight – I believe that this is on account of their diet and general lack of exercise. Everyone drives, in America, and the whole of society is orientated to the motor car. They are all extremely friendly, but in rather a gushing way, not at all like the gentle, quiet friendliness I had encountered amongst the people of Nepal.

Eventually I was on the plane bound for Las Vegas. It was a very comfortable flight, and the food was excellent. As we flew over Las Vegas itself the sight was truly amazing – the lights from all the casinos and hotels lit up the sky so much it seemed just like daylight. At last, twelve hours after leaving Sevenoaks, I found myself in yet another new culture. On the whole, efficiency is the name of the game in the States, but at Las Vegas disaster was to strike. I stood waiting with all the other passengers for my luggage and my bicycle to appear on the slow-moving rubberised conveyor belt, but after we had been waiting for about fifteen minutes, with no sign of anything, the machinery ground to a halt. A steward arrived to announce that the conveyor belt had jammed. It was stuck on a sharp corner, where a mountain of suitcases and bags had piled up, and right underneath this mountain was my poor bicycle! When the problem had been sorted out I was reunited with a very battered-looking machine, that was badly in need of repair.

I made my way to "The Four Queens" hotel/casino, and was welcomed there by the host, Ken Owens. When he discovered what I was up to, he offered me a room for one night, free of charge. As I was only planning to stay one night, and set off the following day for Death Valley, this seemed a great offer – but now, of course, I had to get my bicycle fixed before I could go anywhere, and this forced me to extend my stay a little longer. The following morning my first priority was to find a bicycle shop – not an easy task in a glittering city that is renowned for being the entertainment centre of the world. After many fruitless enquiries, I was eventually told where I would be able to find somewhere I could get the machine fixed. I got into a taxi, and we arrived at the place – only to find the door firmly locked and a notice saying "Open at 10.00 a.m." I looked at my watch. It was 10.15.

"They're late!" I said to the taxi driver. "This shop was supposed to be open at 10.00."

"I'm sorry, Sir," he replied, with the courtesy that is common to all in the States, but trying hard to conceal a smile on his lips. "The time right now is 8.15."

What a fool! I had forgotten to turn my watch back when we entered the state of Nevada. I felt a right charlie, I can tell you.

Anyway, eventually all was sorted; my bicycle was in a fit state once again, and I set off to find the Mayor of the city, Jan Laverty Jones, and hand over my international messages of goodwill. I was also introduced to John Moran, the Sherriff of Las Vegas, and Kenton B. Kirk and Gary Schultz – two biking police sergeants. I had a long, informative and very helpful chat with these two, who gave me some useful advice. They showed me their bicycles, which were equipped with radios and telephones, and were very impressive machines. We had our photographs taken together by the press, and, greatly reasssured by all their encouraging words of wisdom, I at last set off out of the busy city.

Death Valley is situated about 140 miles due west of Las Vegas, in the states of California and Nevada. It was given its rather macabre name in 1849, when the wagon trails in search of gold travelled the route. Many died on the way, and suffered from lack of food and fuel. However, it had been named before this time, by the Shoshone Indians, who are believed to have entered the valley in about AD 1,000. Their name for this inhospitable desert area was *Tomesha*, which means "ground afire". It is a long, narrow valley, some 125 miles long, and between four and sixteen miles wide, and covers nearly 3,000 square miles in area.

It was not long before I was cycling between expanses of desert on either side of the El Camino road. At first one or two houses were scattered about, and I passed several cars, but very soon all sign of human habitation petered out, and the passing vehicles were few and far between. Those that did pass would flash and beep their horns, and wave excitedly at me. A cyclist in America is a rare sight indeed. A cyclist heading in the direction of Death Valley is unheard of! The road was excellent – quite straight – and stretched ahead as far as the eye could see. After about 40 miles the road began to climb, and looking at my map I could see that I was heading for Spring Mountain, a height of 5,000 feet.

The ride to the top was marvellous; a good road, with a steady, even incline, and spectacular views of the colourful rocky out-crops. As I dropped down the other side, I could feel the bike gathering speed; I must have touched about 40 m.p.h. Suddenly I heard the "phut" of something piercing the back wheel; the bike began to wobble precariously, and, aware of the procedure to follow in such an event, I began to apply gentle pressure to the brakes. If you brake suddenly when you have a puncture at high speed you will more than likely crash and fall head-over-heels over the handlebars. I teetered slowly to a halt and looked down at the very miserable sight of a flat back tyre. I had to repair it then and there, of course, and this meant unfastening the carriers from the bike, full of all my gear, and rooting around for the necessary equipment to get the back wheel off and a new inner tube in. I worked quickly, by the side of the road, with the bicycle wheels in the air and all my gear lying about. It must have looked a strange sight to the few motorists who passed by in their large, smooth cars. As I worked away, I noticed a small bird nearby. It was a roadrunner – I recognised it at once from a book I had studied as part of my research into the place – a bird that depends on snakes for its survival. Its appearance here must mean that there were snakes in the vicinity. I had a nervous glance around, but could see nothing, so carried on repairing the bicycle, but working as quickly as I could. When the job was done, I didn't hang about, but got quickly back on the bike and set off once more. Suddenly, just in front of me on the road, I saw two snakes lying quite still. My mind worked quickly as I thought of my possible options. Should I keep going, and cycle around the snakes, thus running the risk of attack? I had visions of them rearing their heads to strike at the bicycle as I passed and becoming entangled in the wheel spokes. Or should I stop, and wait till they went away of their own accord? In the end, I pulled the bike up just before I reached them, and got off. The snakes did not look as if they were going anywhere, and I now felt impatient to continue with my journey, so I took the bicycle pump off the machine and extended it to its full length. I then used this to prod the snakes gently. I was able to push them aside, carefully, and they seemed quite unperturbed. This was to happen several times throughout the trip, and I became quite an expert at the art of snake-defence.

My first overnight stop was at a town called Pahrump. It consisted of a scattering of houses, a small hotel, and the necessary casino. I paid for a room at the hotel, which was pleasant enough, although nothing grand. The Americans have yet to discover the advantages of B & B, and my payment covered only the price of the room. The hotel was run by a couple who engaged me in conversation. They were intrigued to find out what I was doing, and really could not believe that anyone in their right mind would contemplate travelling by bicycle through the desert.

"You must be one of them there eccentric old Englishmen," they proclaimed, unable to conceal their sheer amazement and incredulity. A fairly standard response from all the American people I was to meet along the way. The whole concept of doing anything out of the ordinary, or anything that would require excessive physical exertion, seemed to be totally outside their experience or understanding.

I was up early the following morning, and off again across the desert, making for the settlement of Shoshone, a town named after the Indians who lived there. I hardly saw anyone that day, and began to feel the overwhelming sense of isolation of the desert. Ahead of me, I could see the outline of a mountain range on the horizon, a myriad of soft greens, browns and yellows which contrasted with the harsh light of the desert around. The area of Shoshone is owned by a husband and wife, who are also proprietors of the local store and café.

I was making my way gradually to the southernmost corner of Death Valley, along Highway 127, and heading for Saratoga Spring.

Formed by movements of the earth's surface and enormous rock faults, Death Valley is a huge, narrow, north-south valley more than 140 miles long, but, at its narrowest point, only four miles wide. Salt flats occupy much of the surface area, and the valley floor is often just a vast expanse of dry, cracked, salt-encrusted earth, which looks most inhospitable. Here however, at the southernmost tip of the valley, you encounter unexpected areas of water, and an abundance of plantlife. This is not the main tourist route into the valley: the smooth, wide Route 178 joins through Jubilee Pass some forty miles further north. The route I was on is marked on the map as being suitable for four-wheel drive vehicles only, but I had no problems on my bicycle – I had certainly encountered far worse in the past! The road was somewhat pitted in places, but I was able to remain on the bike through Saratoga Spring, and continue for about 15 miles before I decided to set up camp for the night. I stopped by the side of the road, and checking my exact location on the map found I was precisely o feet above sea level. To my left and right, rocky peaks rose majestically against a pale sky. As the sun began to disappear, I felt the noticeable drop in temperature, and quickly pitched my small tent and began a brew-up on my primus. A sign I had recently passed indicated that flooding was possible in this area. Looking at the flat dry expanse around me, I have to say I found this hard to believe – although it *does* rain in Death Valley, they say, and there can be a sudden change in the appearance of the terrain.

I slept well, that first night in the National Monument (the American equivalent of our National Park) and woke early next morning. Already, the sun was quite high, and the penetrating heat of the day was warming the sides of my tent. After a simple breakfast, I took down the tent and packed up the panniers, ready to be off again and head into the heart of this notorious, and yet ruggedly beautiful valley.

The track I was following joined the main route at a place called Ashford Mill. Here are the first of many ruins which are scattered throughout Death Valley: the ruins of the attempts at civilisation that characterised the valley in the latter half of the previous century.

After the often disastrous forays by the emigrants of 1849, wending their way west in search of fortune, many entrepreneurial prospectors set up home at various locations throughout the valley. Some are more well-known than others, but there are constant reminders of the past undaunted spirit of optimism that led would-be businessmen to create small centres of civilisation and, against all the odds, stake their lives and the lives of their families in search of ore.

Hot enough to fry an egg?

At Ashford Mill, I joined Highway 178, and encountered the ubiquitous evidence of the twentieth century. The road is wide and smooth, and well-maintained, and geared, of course, to the visitor in his motor-vehicle. What all the tourists miss, though, is some of the most spectacular scenery in the States. What they also fail to experience is the true nature of the valley. Closeted in their (often air-conditioned) cars, they cannot hope to feel the effects of the one factor that gave Death Valley its name – the searing, dry heat of the desert.

I was suffering rather more than I might have been, at this point, because of a slight mishap back in Shoshone. I had brought with me a pair of good-quality sun-glasses on the trip, which I had inadvertently dropped, and they had smashed completely. Alas, I had not had the foresight to carry a spare pair, and I thus had to struggle for the next three days with the relentless, glaring

Furnace Creek Visitor Center & one of the exhibits.

light of the sun with its harsh brilliance. The light forced me to adopt a permanent squint, and the brightness gave me a bad headache, for I was forced to keep looking ahead at the road all the time. It was not until I reached Furnace Creek Visitor Center that I was able to purchase another pair of glasses, and I must say I momentarily felt quite grateful for the invasion of the tourist industry.

Furnace Creek is the starting point for most tourist excursions in the Valley. There is a swish hotel here, and a well-equipped camp site. I spent a comfortable night at the latter, and the following morning spent some time wandering around the Center. Palm trees, neatly trimmed lawns, gravelled paths and piped music are the order of the day. It was difficult to realise that we were, in fact, 190 feet below sea level at this point, and in one of the driest places on earth. A museum catalogues the history of Death Valley and displays exhibits of passing interest; anything over fifty years old and it is an antique, to the Americans, and of considerable historical interest. Consequently any old heap of rusting metal has a fence placed around it and an engraved plaque cataloguing its former usefulness.

I did not linger long.

Now fully equipped with sun-glasses I was able to enjoy the ride much more, and I set off northwards once again, along the smooth tarmac of the main south/north route, this time heading for Scottys Castle, some 60 miles on and situated at the northernmost part of Death Valley. The road is flat, and straight, for the most part, and the cycling was not difficult. It was only the heat that made conditions uncomfortable; although I wore a sleeveless vest and shorts for some of the time I had to be cautious because of the dangers of sunburn. It is easy not to notice the strength of the sun, especially when you are cycling and creating a breeze.

It was a lonely journey. I saw very few cars indeed, and there was no one to talk to along the way. I was reminded of the long days cycling all alone through Norway, when I would go for hours without seeing another soul. The terrain round about could not have been more different, however, and at least in Norway when I did stop, there was usually some sign of life about. Even in the most inhospitable areas, you could usually catch sight of Sami farmers, or reindeer herd ambling slowly on, looking for more food. Here the dry heat, the vast flat expanse of the desert, and the bare rocky mountains looming on either side were far more oppressive than the spectacular green mountains and forests of Scandinavia. Everything seemed somehow harsh, in the strong light, and the cars that passed, glinting in the sun, were huge, and flashy, and although they would toot at me I felt it was more because they thought I was such an oddity, rather than because they were being friendly.

Scottys Castle is a large house, or stately home, rather than anything any Englishman would recognize as a castle. With whitewashed walls and red tiled roofing, the turrets and towers look more Mediterranean in appearance than anything else. It was built as the home of one of the more successful prospectors, and is now open to the public as a museum. I am not particularly interested in such things, and, after glancing at the outside, decided not to venture in. I cycled on a few miles, and found a place to camp right on the northernmost border of Death Valley, in the shadow of a range of mountains with the rather ominous and morbid sounding name of "Last Chance Range". There is a wonderful mixture, in the Valley, of original Indian names and their twentieth-century alternatives. The lyrical sounding native names – such as Ubehebe Crater, Mesquite, and Tucki Mountain – are, to my mind, far more imaginative than the rather pedestrian equivalents. Many of these are somewhat alarming, and echo the dramatic intentions of the name of Death Valley itself. You can visit Dry Bone Canyon, Devils Cornfield, Hells Gate, and even the very gruesome sounding Coffin Peak.

Having reached the top of the valley, I now had to retrace my

The dry landscape of Death Valley.

steps, and the next day cycled back down the road for some 50 miles, until I came across a signpost to Stovepipe Wells Village. This road heads west, and takes you past the area known as Devils Cornfield, where arroweed plants grow in unusual clumps that look, from afar, very much like huge haystacks. Stovepipe Wells Village, a few miles beyond the Devils Cornfield, is another purpose-built visitor centre, which has grown from an old mining town that, like all the other settlements of the late nineteenth and early twentieth centuries in Death Valley, did not flourish for very long. Derelict houses and rusty equipment are now glorified by the modern American yearning for a taste of history, and a sense of past identity but far more impressive than the man-made monuments to the past are the majestic natural structures of Death Valley itself. No manner of macabre-sounding names or museums and visitor centres can replace the effect of the topographical features of the landscape, awesome in its stark beauty. Beyond Stovepipe Wells the road begins to rise gradually, and then, after another six miles or so, begins to wind quite sharply upwards. These mountains are nothing compared to the peaks of the Himalayas, but what is most striking is the number of different rock formations. Erosion has created the most unusual shapes and forms within the rock itself; some are smooth and rounded, others are sharp, steep and craggy, and the colours from the various mineral deposits mean that the landscape is constantly changing and often quite breathtaking. As I climbed steadily I was able to catch some really marvellous views, and could see way down below the flat expanse of the valley floor, with a couple of cars crawling like ants along the grey ribbon of road beneath. At Towne Pass (4,956 feet) a roadside sign announced that I was now leaving Death Valley National Monument. Here I stopped for a while, and ate some of the food I had been carrying (army rations, just for a change!) I drank, thirstily, from my two water bottles and rested awhile, before climbing back on the bike and wending my way quite slowly, but very relaxed, back down into the valley. I had to retrace my steps once more, back through Stovepipe Wells and past the Devils Cornfield, and then take the road leading east out of the valley. This road leads along "Mud Canyon" (rather inappropriately named, as far as I could make out) and then to the gruesome sounding Hells Gate, which is in the foothills of the mountains that run along the eastern side of the valley. Beyond Hells Gate the road rises steeply, but far from abandoning hope at this point I have to say that my spirits began to rise, as the air cooled noticeably and I escaped from the relentless dry heat of the valley floor. The rock formations on this side of the valley were, if anything, even more spectacular than those on the western side. The road winds its way quite steeply between outcrops that resemble a lunar landscape – there seemed to be no vegetation at all, for miles. I climbed steadily to the Daylight Pass, some 4,500 feet above sea level. At the top, I stopped to gaze back for the last time at the vast expanse below. The light of the afternoon sun cast long shadows across the valley, and on the eastern slopes around me, the rocks were aflame with a myriad of different hues. There was a stark and rather remote natural beauty about the place. The name Death Valley may conjure up visions of skulls and corpses lying abandoned at the side of the road, but the reality is in fact an area of extraordinary and unusual grandeur. As with the wide forests of Norway, and the majestic peaks of the Himalayas, here was yet another reminder that this earth is a rich and beautiful place to be.

Once down the other side of the mountain range, Route 374 extends in a straight, north-easterly direction across the flat plains of the Nevada desert, to the town of Beatty. I was outside Death Valley now, but the heat was searing and intense, and conditions here certainly no better than in the valley itself. In fact, outside the designated National Monument it is, if anything, more remote and isolated than within the confines of the valley itself. There was a 150-mile ride back to Las Vegas, and this took another day.

Once back, I had to attend a presentation with the Mayor of Las Vagas, Jan Laverty Jones. Although this was to be a formal do, I was asked to attend just as I was. So, amidst all the smart suits of the top notches, I walked up to greet the mayor in the gear I had been wearing for the past five days in the scorching desert heat – with a towel wrapped round my head and track-suit trousers tucked in to my socks. In this garb I had successfully avoided sunburn, and also excited the interest of all those I met. Now I was the cause of much merriment as I was presented, with great honour, with the Key to the City of Las Vegas. A rousing and stirring speech from the mayor praising my achievement as the first person ever to cycle the length and breadth of Death Valley concluded with greetings and good wishes to the people of Kent. Once more I was to be the privileged bearer of goodwill

Not the most welcoming sight for a tired cylist!

between nations. It fills me with immense pride to know that all those long hours spent alone, with just me and my trusty old bicycle (it's still the same old machine; just a few replaced essentials) have touched the hearts and minds of many.

*   *   *   *   *   *

I was back home in time for Christmas. The cold dark days of December in England could not have been a greater contrast to the environment in Death Valley, but as always it was good to be home, and to embark on the rounds of talks and slide shows to remind me of the experiences and relive my days in the desert.

I have been back a few months now. Already I have had the atlas out and have been down to the library on a few occasions,

Still together.

The Hospice at Home team outside Allen Gardiner House.

just undertaking a little investigation. I have a feeling it won't be *too* long before this "Pedalling Pensioner" hits the road again, in search of another challenge.